50p S

PONSFORD
and
WOODFULL

PONSFORD
and
WOODFULL

A Premier Partnership

Marc Fiddian

The Five Mile Press

TO WAL BRIGHT

THE FIVE MILE PRESS
379 Smith Street
Fitzroy Victoria 3065 Australia

First published 1988
© Marc Fiddian
Designed by Patrick Coyle
Edited by Scott Riddle
Printed and bound by South China Printing Company, Hong Kong
Typeset in 11/13 pt Zapf Book Light by
Post Typesetters, Brisbane

National Library of Australia Cataloguing-in-Publication data

Fiddian, Marc.
    Ponsford and Woodfull, a premier partnership.

    Includes index.
    ISBN 0 86788 166 6.

    1. Ponsford, William Harold, 1900–   . 2.
    Woodfull, W. M. (William Maldon), 1897–1965.
    3. Cricket players — Australia — Biography.
    I. Title.

796.35′8′0922

CONTENTS

INTRODUCTION

AUSTRALIAN cricket has produced a number of outstanding opening batsmen since early this century when Victor Trumper and Reg Duff opened the innings in Tests and for New South Wales. Later came distinguished batsmen such as Warren Bardsley and Herbie Collins, followed by the two Victorian right-handers Bill Ponsford and Bill Woodfull. In looking for Australia's finest opening pair one need go no further.

An opening batsman's lot is not an easy one, requiring as it does the skill and patience to blunt an opposition attack and contribute some runs in the process. At times the opener must sacrifice his own game for the good of his team, be it by eliminating a productive but chancy stroke from his repertoire or by sitting back and playing a sheet-anchor role while a free-playing batsman at the other end gathers most of the runs.

Ponsford and Woodfull had the capacity to adapt to the occasion and their different styles made each a good foil for the other. Ponsford made his runs more quickly, using an attacking range of strokes, but Woodfull had a superb defence and once settled was a hard man to shift. Each had tremendous concentration and Ponsford's capacity to bat for long periods was extraordinary.

Although their batting differed, the careers of the two players followed a parallel course. Woodfull, three years older than Ponsford, first played with Victoria in 1922. Ponsford, after one appearance in 1921, had to wait two years and hit a world record score to seal

7

his place. He won Test selection in the 1924–25 series against England, but Woodfull had to wait until 1926. Ponsford finished his Test career with a batting average of 48.23. Woodfull's was 46.00. In first-class games Ponsford averaged 65.18 and Woodfull 64.99. Woodfull, who played 10 more innings, hit 49 centuries to Ponsford's 47. Each retired in November 1934.

While there were similarities in ability and run yield, there were areas where one outshone the other. Woodfull went much further as a captain, a role he played with distinction for both Australia and Victoria. Ponsford captained St Kilda and occasionally led Victorian teams, but didn't show the same flair. Twice Woodfull won back the Ashes on a tour of England, a unique feat.

Apart from their many big partnerships together, it was Ponsford who showed the propensity to venture into scoring of gigantic proportions. Had he confined his record-making to one massive partnership or one individual score of 400, then he would be remembered as an outstanding player. But 'Ponny' twice hit more than 400 in an innings — a record even Bradman couldn't beat — and was involved in four huge partnerships with batsmen other than Woodfull. They were 456 with Edgar Mayne for the first wicket, 451 with Bradman for the second wicket, 389 with Stan McCabe for the third wicket and 388 with Bradman for the fourth wicket. The two stands with Bradman were in Tests.

For more than a decade Ponsford was one of the world's finest batsmen and at times he strode the cricket scene like a colossus. Had it not been for the emergence of Don Bradman while Ponsford was at his peak, the Victorian's accomplishments would have shone through the succeeding eras with an even brighter light. While Bradman overshadowed Ponsford with his freakish scoring feats, 'Ponny' was the one player who could bat in tandem with 'The Don' and display the same aplomb.

Of the 10 highest scores made in Sheffield Shield games, the first, fifth and eighth belong to Bradman. The second, seventh and ninth were hit by Ponsford. Another measure of Ponsford's brilliance was that he hit four first-class scores of more than 300, a record to rival Bradman's six. Bob Simpson hit two triple centuries — within 12 months of each other — and such cricketing giants as Clem Hill, Victor Trumper, Warwick Armstrong and Charlie Macartney did it once. Among some very fine players who didn't hit a triple century in first-class games were Woodfull, whose highest score was 284, Greg Chappell (247 not out), Ian Chappell (209), Bill Lawry (266), Doug Walters (253) and Neil Harvey (231).

Evaluating the worth of Ponsford and Woodfull is not easy in view of changes to the game in the past century or more. The two Victorians certainly had the benefit of batting on some fine pitches, prepared to last, but they also had the disadvantage of playing on uncovered pitches which became a batsman's nightmare after heavy rain. In particular, a Melbourne 'sticky' was horrendous.

These days more Test matches are played than in the 1920s and 1930s, and batting records, even Bradman's, are being beaten. However the modern player usually needs twice the number of innings to run up scores comparable to Bradman's. The one common denominator we can call on to draw comparisons is the player's average. Here of course Bradman stands alone, with 95.14 in first-class games. Vijay Merchant, the Indian champion of the 30s and 40s, finished with 71.33 and George Headley, of the West Indies, earned 69.86. Of the other batsmen to distinguish themselves by averaging more than 60, Ponsford (65.18) and Woodfull (64.99) complete this elite band.

Ponsford was without peer against spin bowling. Some of the most talented slow men said they preferred to bowl to Bradman because they felt they had some chance of dismissing him whereas 'Ponny' gave them none. As a result, a myth has grown that Ponsford was never stumped. Actually he was out this way 10 times in his 235 first-class innings, but for a batsman who ventured down the pitch so often it is remarkable that he was stumped on so few occasions.

Robustly built and sometimes referred to as 'Puddin', Ponsford paid strict attention to correct use of his feet and didn't worry about being stumped. His positive approach meant that he was invariably to the pitch of the ball and had it well covered. The late A.G. 'Johnny' Moyes, a fine judge of a cricketer, described Ponsford as a master of slow bowling, almost infallible against spin because he seemed to know just what spin had been imparted by the bowler.

The talented English batsman and athlete Charles Fry said of Ponsford: 'He reminds me of a good, short-legged hunter galloping well within his powers. He hits beautifully on the off-side off his back foot, and drives hard and straight on the on and off. By running out close to the pitch of the ball he hunts down the ball with quick close-coupled steps and feet near together. At the instant of impact the ball hums.'

Batting with Ponsford in a Victorian match in the early 1930s, Leo O'Brien was impressed by a particular aspect of his partner's footwork and during a break in play he asked where 'Ponny' had learned. 'I once fielded at fine leg during a long innings by Jack

Hobbs and took the chance to study his footwork,' Ponsford explained.

Ponsford will be remembered for his choice of a heavy bat, referred to as 'Big Bertha', which weighed 1.18 kg (2 lb 10 oz). He liked the heavy bat although he pointed out there was no hard and fast rule as to a heavier batsman using a heavy bat and a lighter player choosing a light blade. A big man might be happy with a 2 lb 2 oz bat and a small player might be comfortable with a 2 lb 6 oz blade, he explained.

While people like to remember Ponsford as the batsman who was never stumped, others think of Woodfull as the man who was never bowled. Woodfull, who batted with a short backlift and kept his bat close to the ground, was sometimes known as 'the worm-killer' as a result. His short backlift and tight defence, more in line with the technique employed by English openers, earned him the reputation of 'the unbowlable' early in his career, but in all he was bowled 72 times in 245 first-class innings.

Former England captain and Middlesex all-rounder Walter Robins said of Woodfull in a *Wisden* obituary: 'Only once did I have the distinction of getting him out — at Lord's in the second Test in 1930. By then he had made 155 and I think he fell through sheer exhaustion. As a man he was very kindly and as a batsman he had a wonderful defence.'

Apart from his batting, Woodfull showed great skill as a captain. Former Victorian and Test batsman Leo O'Brien described Woodfull as 'an unforgettable man. His character and courage were unforgettable and his captaincy instilled a determination in others to do well.'

Woodfull, who earned great respect from his players, ranks among the finest to lead Australia. Unless a player sought advice Woodfull did not tell him how he should play. Once a player had attained Test status he was expected to know the game thoroughly. Woodfull's captaincy was largely by example although as a teetotaller he was not averse to team mates having a drink. His ability to extract the best from each player enabled the team to run itself. 'He had an iron fist but he did not have to use it,' observed O'Brien.

Between them, Ponsford and Woodfull formed a formidable opening partnership and made a considerable contribution to cricket, not to mention the entertainment they brought to the game's many followers.

EARLY DAYS

AMONG the many towns in Victoria that owe their existence to the discovery of gold, Maldon has become one of the more famous because of the National Trust's classification of the whole town. Situated on the slopes of Mount Tarrangower, 136 kilometres north-west of Melbourne, the town was named Maldon in 1856 — three years after the discovery of gold. The settlement grew to the extent that a branch railway was built from the nearby town of Castlemaine and the various aspects that mark a permanent township were established.

In 1897 the Reverend Thomas Staines Brittingham Woodfull was appointed minister of the Methodist church in Maldon after serving at Port Cygnet (Tasmania) and earlier at Kerang in northern Victoria. Although born in Australia, Woodfull's forebears had lived in Warwickshire before members of the family migrated to Australia and the United States. Thomas Woodfull and his wife had seven children, one of whom — daughter Vera — died in infancy. Bill, born at Maldon on August 22, 1897 was named William Maldon Woodfull. The third of four sons, his elder brothers were Balfour and Melville and his younger brother was Colin. He also had an elder sister Dora and a younger sister Faith.

Bill Woodfull was born in the spring of 1897, shortly before Essendon — the Australian Rules football club he was to follow — won the initial Victorian Football League (VFL) premiership and Amberite, a son of the champion horse Carbine, won the AJC Derby, Caulfield Cup and Victoria Derby. Following those notable events the Australian cricket team, under Harry Trott, scored a 4–1 win against the touring

11

Englishmen. A 20-year-old South Australian, Clem Hill, scored his maiden Test century and Monty Noble played his first Test during the series. Both men, like Bill Woodfull, were destined to captain Australia.

The 1897–98 summer was a particularly hot one in Victoria — Melbourne recorded 16 centuries (38 degrees Celsius) — and raising a young family without the help of a refrigerator or air conditioner tested the fortitude of a mother. The Woodfulls did not have a long stay in Maldon, shifting to Shepparton in 1901 and then to Melbourne in 1904 where the family lived at 165 Mount Alexander Road, Flemington, followed by several years in East Melbourne. Later the family moved to Bendigo and then back to Melbourne in 1914, residing at 7 Lyndhurst Crescent, Hawthorn.

As he grew up W.M. Woodfull preferred to be called Bill, rather than 'Maldy', a contraction of Maldon, which his family tended to use. Once he reached the Victorian cricket XI he was definitely Bill[1]. After Melbourne High School, Bill Woodfull attended Teachers Training College and then the University of Melbourne, where he gained a Bachelor of Arts degree and a Diploma of Education. A very competent tennis player, he also played football with University as a half-back flanker who kicked with the left foot.

Owing to the Great War, Melbourne's District cricket competition was suspended from 1915–18 although clubs continued to play one another on a regular basis. In 1916–17 Woodfull, whose family had shifted from Hawthorn to Moonee Ponds, played with Essendon and gained selection in the first XI on half a dozen occasions. An unbeaten 24 against Northcote in his first game and 12 against Prahran were his only double-figure scores. The following season he was down in the seconds and one can only assume that he put his studies before everything else, not taking cricket particularly seriously. A boyhood attack of rheumatic fever had left him stiff-jointed and this undoubtedly retarded his development as a batsman.

Woodfull attracted real attention as a cricketer in 1920, the year of his first appointment as a teacher (to Maryborough High School in central Victoria). It was at Maryborough, not so distant from his birthplace Maldon, that he began to score a lot of runs at huge averages because he was rarely dismissed. Victoria's selectors jotted down his name. A game with the State Colts or the second XI was in order to see just how much promise he had.

While Bill Woodfull was a relative latecomer to cricket, his famous partner couldn't make the grade quickly enough. Born at 82 Newry Street, North Fitzroy (an inner Melbourne suburb), on October 19

1900, William Harold Ponsford was the oldest of four children. A brother, Ray[2], and sisters Dorothy and Ida completed the family. His father Bill was a postal worker and his grandfather, also Bill, had a carrying business, being described at the time as a 'van proprietor'. Grandfather Ponsford, born in Devon circa 1839, had been a tin miner before coming to Australia on the ship 'Suffolk' in 1862. He settled at Sandhurst (later Bendigo) where he married in 1869. His wife died and he remarried in 1873. He set up business as a carrier between Sandhurst and North Melbourne and lived until 1905.

W.H. Ponsford was born the day before Ingliston won the 1900 Caulfield Cup and 10 weeks before the federation of the Australian colonies. It was the year Theodore Dreiser's controversial but brilliant novel, 'Sister Carrie', was published and the 64th year of Queen Victoria's reign. There were no Test matches in the season of Ponsford's birth, but Victoria won the inter-state Sheffield Shield.

Melbourne, a growing city of more than half a million people, became the temporary capital of Australia at Federation and the ornate buildings that studded the city centre reflected the importance of the metropolis. Railways stretched to the outer suburbs and, closer to town, cable trams trundled along Rathdowne Street to North Carlton, along Nicholson Street to Park Street in North Fitzroy and along Brunswick Street to St George's Road in the same suburb. As a baby, Ponsford lived at 391 Station Street North Carlton, and in boyhood at 408 Station Street.

It was at nearby Alfred Crescent State School, North Fitzroy, that the future champion began to show great promise with a cricket bat. He also showed a distinct flair for baseball and at the age of 14 represented a Victorian State Schools team against New South Wales in Sydney. Later he played baseball with Fitzroy and later still with Melbourne, when matches were played as curtain-raisers to VFL football. Regarded as one of the best baseballers in Australia, Ponsford excelled as a catcher and at one stage was approached to play in the United States by John 'Mugsy' McGraw, manager of the New York Giants. Ponsford wasn't interested.

As a schoolboy Ponsford was most enthusiastic about learning the skills of cricket, so much so that he would run from school through the Edinburgh Gardens to the Fitzroy Cricket Ground to be first at club practice. In both 1913–14 and 1914–15 he was one of the club's schoolboy medallion winners, which entitled him to practise with the top players[3]. One player to impress the youngster was Les Cody, a very well-equipped strokemaker who eventually hit eight centuries for Fitzroy and played 30 first-class games.

13

The Fitzroy ground in busy Brunswick Street had none of the spaciousness of the Melbourne Cricket Ground (MCG) and could be most uncomfortable when accommodating a large football crowd. More in keeping with a cricket ground in England's industrial north than the dual-purpose Australian sports ground, the Fitzroy ground nevertheless had a charm that encapsulated the fervent support that Melburnians gave their local sports teams. Two identical grandstands, replete with fancy iron lace along the balustrades, faced south — ideal for watching cricket when the summer sun or a hot northerly was at its fiercest.

Young Ponsford set about perfecting the art of batsmanship. Any hopes held by the Fitzroy Club that he would one day play in the first XI were dashed when his father was appointed supervisor of letter carriers at Elsternwick post office and the family shifted residence to 22 Orrong Road, Elsternwick. This meant that Bill was bound by residential rules to play district cricket with St Kilda when the time came.

Ponsford's natural ability earned him a place in the St Kilda first XI in the opening game of the 1916–17 season. He was still 15, five days short of his 16th birthday. By coincidence the match was against Fitzroy at Fitzroy, the ground he used to rush to after school for cricket practice and in winter would watch football matches from the balcony of his aunt's home, when Jimmy Freake was the Fitzroy team's star full-forward and Percy Parratt, Tom Heaney and Jim Toohey formed a crack half-forward line.

Chris Kiernan, a former Fitzroy footballer of note and an all-round sportsman, bowled Ponsford for 12 in his first game for St Kilda, but the team's total was only 116 and they kept him in the team. Later in the season he showed fine defence in making 25 against Collingwood before being caught off Jack Ryder. St Kilda officials believed the experience was good for the lad and the following season he hit his first half century, a valuable 60 at Essendon, before being run out. Although he gave several chances along the way, the outfield was slow and his innings did not contain a boundary. St Kilda, with a total of 179, won the game by 11 runs. Against University, Ponsford opened the bowling and took two wickets. In later years an over from 'Ponny' was very rare.

Meanwhile, Ponsford had left school to attend Hassett's business college in Chapel Street, Prahran. 'My father said it was to freshen me up,' he recalled in 1985. From Hassett's he gained a job with the State Savings Bank at its head office in Elizabeth Street Melbourne.

In 1918–19 his batting began to mature. That season's aggregate of 483 included a hand of 95 and two other half-centuries. When play resumed after the Christmas break, Ponsford hit 87 in a St Kilda score of eight for 197 against Carlton. For more than three hours he was untroubled by the bowling and the *Argus* newspaper described his effort as 'a good but not faultless' innings. Although only 18, he was then chosen to play for Victoria against Tasmania in Hobart. Other members of the team included Arthur Liddicut, Jack Ellis and Fred Yeomans. Selection in the team was a big break for those aspiring to play Sheffield Shield cricket but, unfortunately for those concerned, the game, due to be played early in February 1919, was cancelled due to an Australia-wide pneumonic influenza epidemic.

Early the following season, at South Melbourne, Ponsford and Bert Cohen gave their side a start worth 194. The players, who were destined to share a number of big partnerships, made 94 and 91 respectively. Overall, Ponsford slipped on his 1918–19 form. This would have been due largely to rival teams building up strength after the war. Despite the drop in his average, Ponsford's talent had been noticed and a place in the Victorian team wasn't far off.

NOTES

[1]Former Australian Prime Minister Sir Robert Menzies once joked about Bill Woodfull's middle name, saying, 'How lucky that my parents didn't christen me Robert Jeparit Menzies.' Woodfull replied, 'May I assure the Prime Minister that Maldon is no more euphonious than Jeparit.'

[2]Ray Ponsford played Sub-District cricket with Elsternwick as a bowler.

[3]Neil Harvey, the most famous Fitzroy player and a Test representative 79 times from 1947–48 to 1962–63, said in his biography *My World of Cricket* that Fitzroy's medallion scheme was an incentive to local schoolboys to join the club. 'This medallion entitled the lucky boy to share in all the facilities of the Fitzroy club for that particular year, including the right to practise at the club nets with the leading players.'

THE CURTAIN RISES

TEST cricket returned to Australia in 1920–21 after a nine-year absence and, under Warwick Armstrong's captaincy, the home side made a clean sweep of the series against Johnny Douglas's English tourists. Strengthened by the inclusion of such players as Herbie Collins and Jack Gregory, Australia won all five Tests in a resounding display of cricket skills.

During the third Test in Adelaide, Armstrong severely bruised a leg, which ultimately caused his withdrawal from the Sheffield Shield game against New South Wales in Sydney. Hopeful that the injury would not prevent his playing in the 100th game between the two States, Armstrong went to Sydney intending to captain Victoria. Shortly before the game was due to start Armstrong consulted his vice-captain, Edgar Mayne, and team-mate Dr Roy Park and it was agreed that 'The Big Ship'[1] would be better off resting the leg to make sure he was fit for the fourth Test.

It seems the Victorian manager was not told of the reason for Armstrong's withdrawal and this, coupled with the big fellow's visit to Randwick racecourse a day or two later, caused the Victorian selectors to omit him from the team to play the visiting MCC in Melbourne a week later. So incensed was the public that protest meetings were held outside the MCG, at the Athenaeum Theatre and at the Melbourne Town Hall.

Following the Shield match in Sydney, in which indifferent batting by Victoria in the first innings led to a four-wicket loss, selectors Ernie Bean, Peter McAlister and Matt Ellis made a number of other

Bill Ponsford... a taciturn man whose run-scoring feats started a new era in major cricket.

Bill Woodfull: perhaps the most respected Australian cricketer of all time. His batting also was of an exceptionally high standard.

i

Bill Ponsford's birth place, 82 Newry Street, North Fitzroy. Twenty-five years later he hit a century for Victoria against Western Australia on the Fitzroy ground, only a block away.

Main Street, Maldon is famous for being classified by the National Trust. It is also notable because author Henry Handel Richardson (Ethel Florence Richardson) lived at the post office as a girl and Bill Woodfull was born at this Victorian midlands town.

changes to the team. Notable were the inclusion of Bill Ponsford in his first-class debut and Prahran spinner Clarrie Grimmett, who took the place of Bert Ironmonger.

The match began on Friday, February 4 1921. Victoria made 268. Jack Ryder contributed 54 and Ponsford, batting at number five, made six before being caught at point off Frank Woolley. A contemporary report said of the new batsman, 'Ponsford opened carefully. He crouches at the wicket but showed he can hit by beautifully driving a ball from Douglas to the off boundary.'

In his second innings Ponsford batted at number six and had made 19 when a ball from Percy Fender beat him. Wicketkeeper Dolphin removed the bails in what was to prove an unusual way of dismissing Ponsford. Ryder's 108 helped Victoria reach 295, but the MCC was untroubled, winning by seven wickets after making 486 in its first innings thanks to a mighty 271 from 'Patsy' Hendren.

Ponsford was unlucky. Victoria had completed its four Shield games for the season, so it was back to club games and more hard work to win recognition for his talent. St Kilda headed the Victorian Cricket Association (VCA) ladder from Prahran at the end of the season, but in the final Prahran proved the better side. St Kilda made 285, which appeared to be a winning score, but Prahran made light of the big target, finally making 5 for 387. Ponsford contributed 18 to his side's total and finished 15th in the VCA averages with 386 runs at an average of 42.88 per innings.

Meanwhile, Bill Woodfull had taken a big step forward by playing a commendable innings for a Ballarat XV against the MCC. Batting for almost three hours he made a chanceless 51 before being caught at the wicket off Wilfred Rhodes. In the second innings he managed only one run, but he was not alone. There were six ducks and the locals totalled a mere 30. Woolley and Fender each hit a century for the Englishmen, Fender scoring a six and a duck off the same stroke in the strangest of incidents. Alan Young, of Ballarat, takes up the description: 'Fender hit the biggest six I've ever seen. It cleared the Ebden Street fence of the Eastern Oval, landed in a fowlyard and killed a duck.'

The following season Woodfull's form in Maryborough was so good that he was chosen to play for Victoria Colts against South Australia Colts at the MCG early in December 1921. The Victorian team was captained by L.F. Freemantle, of University, and all players except Woodfull were from Melbourne clubs. Ponsford, who had continued to bat steadily with St Kilda without advancing to huge scores, also gained inclusion.

Woodfull was called on to open the Victorian innings and made 14 before being trapped lbw by Gray, a left-arm medium pace bowler. Ponsford, used down the list, batted soundly and quickly, compiling 41 in 51 minutes. Strangely enough he hit only one boundary and 11 singles in an innings that ended when he stepped back to a delivery from Gray, missed in his attempt to punch it through the field and was bowled. Gray finished with six for 63 in a Victorian total of 254, to which the South Australians replied with 129.

Victoria's second innings began with a blaze of runs from Woodfull and Fitzroy batsman James 'Snowy' Atkinson[2]. Atkinson was the more attacking player as the partnership gained stature, while Woodfull seemed content to build his score with singles. Atkinson was out for 125 with the total at 194, after which it was Woodfull's turn to complete a century. When he reached 68 Woodfull had made 29 successive singles, which reflected the caution and restraint of his batting. Later in the innings he opened out and played his strokes with much skill.

Woodfull's score climbed way past the century and at the fall of the fourth wicket he was joined by Ponsford in an unbroken stand. The Maryborough batsman left the field with 186 not out to his name and his St Kilda colleague was 44 not out in a team score of four for 399. A formidable partnership had taken root.

Freemantle declared the Victorian second innings closed at the overnight score and the home side dismissed South Australia for 183 to win the game by 341 runs.

That month Woodfull completed his term at Maryborough High School and prepared to move back to Melbourne to take up an appointment at Williamstown High School. His parents, meanwhile, had shifted to South Melbourne which meant Bill would be residentially bound to play District cricket with South, a club whose reputation was to be enhanced by his few years there.[3]

Following his 200 runs for once out with the Victorian Colts, Woodfull was chosen to play in the Victorian second XI against New South Wales seconds at the MCG towards the end of January 1922. Ponsford was also in the side. Victoria batted first, with Woodfull and Keith Tolhurst opening the innings. Before long Victoria had lost three wickets for 30 runs, but George Davies, a left-hander from Essendon, joined Woodfull and each scored a century. Their stand of 197 took only 134 minutes. Other batsmen, including Ponsford, who hit eight, joined Woodfull. The latter played confidently towards a double century. Eventually he carried his bat, being 227 not out when the last wicket fell at 439. Woodfull's batting was described by *The Age* as 'more solid than brilliant' and his big score included 22 fours.

New South Wales replied with 516, offering much resistance towards the end of the innings. Ponsford and Woodfull were both called on to bowl, 'Woody' ending the innings of top-scorer Oswald Asher for 119. In the time remaining Victoria hit 6 for 190, of which Ponsford at number six, and batting for an hour, contributed a bright 51 not out. Woodfull joined him at number eight and was 20 not out when the game finished. This meant that Woodfull had been dismissed only once in scoring 447 runs for Victorian minor teams.

Immediately after the seconds game, Woodfull hit 63 for his new VCA club against Northcote and followed with an unbeaten 156 in South Melbourne's score of five for 290 (dec.) against Essendon. Woodfull batted relatively briskly, being at the crease for 220 minutes, and hit 16 fours. 'One seriously wonders what will occur if he and (Roy) Park get set,' commented *The Age*.

Woodfull was rewarded for his efforts with a place in the Victorian team to play South Australia in Adelaide in its final Shield engagement for the season. The team was also to play Western Australia in Perth. At this stage Victoria had already won the Shield and underlined its strength by beating the South Australians by an innings, despite the absence of its best fast man, Ted McDonald. The match was not a memorable first-class debut for 'Woody', who split a hand while fielding and scored 22 not out at number eight, contributing only marginally to Victoria's massive total of 625. Frank O'Keefe[3], who opened with Edgar Mayne, top-scored with 180.

In Perth the same opening partnership was used after skipper Mayne won the toss and batted. The first wicket yielded 100 before O'Keefe (41) was out and Woodfull joined Mayne. The pair pushed the score to 150 when Mayne was out for 73. By stumps Woodfull was still there on 122, having completed his maiden first-class century. The next day he proceeded to 153 before being run out and the Victorian score advanced from five for 335 to all out at 485. The home State, which was destined to wait until 1947–48 for admittance to the Shield competition, made 245 and 168 in reply. Fast bowler Percy Wallace, who had been playing with Prahran seconds at the start of the season, took eight for 67 in Western Australia's first innings.

On returning to Melbourne, Bill Woodfull maintained his impressive form when South Melbourne ran into trouble against Hawthorn-East Melbourne. Chasing 196, the Southerners had lost four for 31 before a fifth-wicket stand worth 157 between Woodfull and Park swung the game. The partnership occupied only 107 minutes, Park finishing with 114 and Woodfull 84. *The Age* said of the effort, 'Without doubt Woodfull is a class batsman. He watches the ball very closely and places very cleverly, particularly on the on-side.'

At Toorak Park on the same day there was a similar situation, with St Kilda in trouble at three for 33 before a century partnership between Ponsford and Reg Ellis lifted the Saints to a 15-run win. Ponsford's 64 was his highest score with St Kilda for the season.

Shortly before Woodfull had made his Victorian debut, 'Ponny' had represented Victoria against Tasmania in Launceston and hit his first century in first-class cricket. Used as a lower order batsman he made 162 in a Victorian score of 550. His effort received relatively little recognition although the noted weekly, *The Australasian*, said the innings 'greatly advanced his claims for Sheffield Shield representation'. The bat used by Ponsford to make his runs had been rejected by most St Kilda first XI players at the start of the season, but it suited 'Ponny' and he was still using it a year later when he scored 429 against Tasmania.

NOTES

[1]Warwick Armstrong, an outstanding all-rounder who played 50 Tests for Australia, was known as 'The Big Ship' because of his immense size. He stood 6 feet 3 inches (191cm) and weighed 21 stone (133kg). His huge shirt and boots remain at the MCG as museum pieces.

[2]Atkinson, also a VFL footballer of note with Fitzroy, played four matches in the Victorian XI and later captained Tasmania. In first-class games he scored a total of 1408 runs at an average of 32.74 and hit two centuries.

[3]Woodfull became the fourth of seven South Melbourne players to captain Australia in Test matches. The others were John Blackham, Warwick Armstrong, Harry Trott, Lindsay Hassett, Ian Johnson, and Graham Yallop. An eighth player, Keith Miller, deputised for Johnson in a 1955 Test in the West Indies, when Johnson was injured.

[4]O'Keefe had come to Melbourne from Sydney that season and showed remarkable form in making 87 and 79 against New South Wales, 180 against South Australia and 177 and 141 for the Rest of Australia versus the Australian XI in Frank Iredale's testimonial match. Tragically he died in London from peritonitis in 1924, aged 27. Had he lived he would have continued his first-class career with Lancashire.

FOUR HUNDREDS
IN ONE

THE prospect of holding a world record before the season ended would not have entered Bill Ponsford's mind when he began the 1922–23 season with innings of 15 and 56 not out against University. The possibility of earning a place in the Victorian XI was growing, but Ponsford badly needed a run of good scores to convince the selectors that he was worthy of advancement.

Early in the season, on November 4 and 11 at South Melbourne, the two Bills were opposed in a drawn game but one in which each played a significant hand. South batted first and made a solid 265 and Woodfull contributed 61 in 131 minutes, with some fine off-driving marking his display. St Kilda was 4 for 239 when the game ended. Ponsford seemed certain of reaching his first District century but was run out for 99 from a good return by Woodfull. *The Age* described Ponsford's innings as a masterful display. Batting for only 113 minutes, he hit nine fours and shared a second-wicket stand of 109 with Doug Hotchin.

Despite being bowled for zero in the next game, against North Melbourne, and then making a duck against Northcote, Ponsford was 12th man for Victoria against a visiting MCC side captained by Archie MacLaren the next month. MacLaren, then at the end of his cricketing career, hit the then highest score in first-class cricket in 1895, when he made 424 for Lancashire against Somerset.

In a relatively low-scoring game, Victoria won by two wickets, with Woodfull's first innings hand of 74 a vital factor in the win. After the MCC had been dismissed for a modest 210 in its first innings, Victoria was in much trouble at 5 for 44 by stumps. A sixth-wicket partnership of 144 between Woodfull and Albert Hartkopf rescued the State and enabled it to compile a useful 278. Woodfull, who batted for an hour and a half before hitting his first boundary, had been at the crease for 165 minutes for his 74 when he was run out by a brilliant piece of fielding by Percy Chapman.

Hartkopf, who top-scored with 86, proved his ability as an all-rounder by taking eight for 105 in the MCC's second innings, which ended at 231. Needing only 164 to win, Victorian captain Edgar Mayne kept back Woodfull and Hartkopf until they were most needed. Woodfull joined Hartkopf when six runs were required to win and was four not out at the finish. Victoria had lost eight wickets along the way. On December 23 Victoria, the Sheffield Shield holder, began its defence of the title against New South Wales at the MCG. The only other Shield game played that season had been in Adelaide, where New South Wales had beaten South Australia by an innings and 310 runs after making a massive score of 786. Four players — Alan Kippax, Johnny Taylor, Hunter Hendry and Bert Oldfield — had made centuries, Kippax's 170 being the finest hand.

Rain made batting difficult in the Melbourne match. New South Wales batted first and, despite a resolute 68 from Kippax, was all out for 160. Woodfull (47) and Mayne (24) gave Victoria a sound start, but the innings was wound up abruptly when Charlie Macartney came on as the number five bowler and took five for 8 off 5.6 overs with his spinners.

In its second innings New South Wales managed only 141. Arthur Liddicut was Victoria's best bowler, finishing with four wickets for 39. A painstaking 84 not out by Woodfull, including only two fours and occupying three and a half hours, swung the game in Victoria's second innings. Park was 30 not out when Victoria reached three for 178 to win by seven wickets.

Meanwhile, the second XIs of the two States were opposed and Ponsford made good use of the game with scores of 37 and 72. Also playing for Victoria in that game was Prahran spin bowler Clarrie Grimmett, who took three for 95.

On returning from the second XI's game, played in Sydney, players were emphatic that Ponsford should be one of the first men selected in the Victorian team. Ponsford recalled in 1985 that St Kilda officials were constantly at odds with VCA secretary Ernie Bean, who was also one of the three State selectors, and treasurer Harry Rush. The fact that Ponsford was a St Kilda player rather than a Melbourne, East Melbourne or South Melbourne representative could well have weighed against him.

In the first round of District games after Christmas, Woodfull hit 12 against Collingwood and Ponsford made 13 against Prahran at Toorak Park, to be stumped off the bowling of Grimmett, who took the first six wickets and finished with eight for 82 in a total of 228. Their individual scores were again almost identical in the next round, when Ponsford showed excellent timing and cover-driving to make 98 in only two hours against Richmond, while Woodfull hit 93 against Hawthorn-East Melbourne at Glenferrie. For the first time since returning from Maryborough, in either District or first-class games, Woodfull was bowled. The successful bowler was H.S. Gamble, who subsequently appeared for Victoria with little note.

When Victoria's selectors chose a team of prospective Shield players to meet Tasmania they gave the captaincy to Ponsford. The match, exactly two years after Ponsford had made his debut with Victoria against the MCC, was played at the MCG. Bearing in mind that Ponsford, then only 22, was starting his third first-class match, the events that followed were extraordinary.

At stumps on the first day, a Friday, Victoria was one for 166 in reply to Tasmania's 217. Ponsford batted at number five and at lunch on Saturday was 25 not out. By tea he was 121 and at stumps had accelerated his run-scoring to be unbeaten on 234 in a total of five wickets for 672. Sunday was a rest day and as captain it was up to Ponsford whether to close the innings or to bat on. He decided on the latter.

Determined to gather as many runs as possible, Ponsford spent most of the Monday breaking records. First he broke Armstrong's record for Victoria in an interstate game (250), then he beat Victor Trumper's highest score in an interstate game (292 not out). At lunch Ponsford was 375, having added 141 in the day's first session. Soon after resuming his epic innings, 'Ponny' passed Charlie Gregory's Australian record of 383 for New South Wales against Queensland.

One record remained, but it wasn't long before it, too, fell. MacLaren's world record first-class score of 424 for Lancashire against Somerset, dating back to 1895, was surpassed as the Victorian total neared 1000. L.T. Mullett, who was also heading for his highest first-class score (16), had strike on 999 but sportingly played out the over to give his partner the honor of bringing up the 1000. Having batted 477 minutes for 429 runs, Ponsford had conquered the world and went for the big hit. Tasmanian Bert Davie, later to cross Bass Strait and serve Prahran with distinction, caught the record-breaker off Allen's bowling at 1001. At nine for 1002, when Mullett was out, Ponsford allowed the final two batsmen the chance to share in the glory while he gave his feet a well-earned rest.

Tailenders Gamble and Lansdown added a further 57 before the Victorian innings was wound up for 1059, made in only 641 minutes and eclipsing the previous highest first-class innings of 918 set by New South Wales against South Australia at the SCG in 1900–01.

Ponsford, the quiet State Savings Bank clerk, had shown singular concentration and application in compiling his 429, which included 42 boundaries. Even for a physically fit young man, he had displayed amazing stamina to keep going for so long.

Dismissed about half an hour before tea, Ponsford was a public hero in a matter of hours. The St Kilda City Council met that night and the mayor, Burnett Gray, delighted that it was a St Kilda player who had made the biggest achievement, moved that a letter of congratulation be sent to Ponsford. Ponsford's employer gave him a gold watch and chain to mark the achievement and the VCA presented him with a miniature gold bat.

MacLaren saw the matter in a different light. His world record had been beaten, but rather than acknowledge the fact he wrote to Ponsford querying the first-class status of the match. Certainly Victoria had not picked its best team and the Tasmanian bowling was not as strong as that of New South Wales or South Australia, but the match had been played over the statutory three days by two States with first-class status. Any record was available to any player as long as he was good enough, and Ponsford proved that he had the capacity to bat beyond the confines of the average player.

Apart from Ponsford's quadruple century, Carlton batsman 'Hammy' Love hit 156 and helped 'Ponny' add 336 for the fifth wicket. Ponsford and W.H. Bailey, who hit 82, then put on 197 for the sixth wicket, followed by a stand of 164 with Karl Schneider (55) for the seventh wicket.

When Tasmania eventually batted a second time, it was all out for 176. Victoria had won by an innings and 666 runs and a new batting star had arrived.

Ponsford's selection for Victoria's final Sheffield Shield match of the season (against South Australia in Adelaide), and against MacLaren's touring MCC side, became a formality. En-route to Adelaide, the Victorian team played a two-day game against a Ballarat XV at Ballarat's Eastern Oval. The locals, with the luxury of 15 batsmen (although only 11 players fielded), made 201 of which Dr Curtis hit 89. Bill Woodfull and Collingwood batsman Les Keating opened for Victoria, being parted at 26 when Keating was out for 12. Woodfull hit 40, Arthur Liddicut 100 and Ponsford was run out for 52 in

Victoria's score of 414. The locals were eight for 130 in their second innings.

The Adelaide game was notable in that the proceeds were given to the George Giffen testimonial fund. To mark the occasion the great left-hand batsman Clem Hill came out of retirement to captain South Australia. At the age of 45 Hill wasn't expected to be up to his former standard, but he still found enough skill to play useful innings of 66 and 39.

Hampden Love and fast bowler Tom Carlton were included in the Victorian team. With Ponsford they made a significant contribution to their side's seven-wicket win. Ponsford, batting at number five, signalled the start of his prolific Shield career by making 108 in Victoria's first innings score of 386. Woodfull, who opened with Love, hit 123 and the South Australian bowlers were given some indication of what could be expected if the two Bills hit form together.

Trailing by 111 on the first innings, South Australia managed 303 in its second visit to the crease due to a brilliant knock of 152 by J.T. Murray. Carlton eventually bowled Murray and finished with five for 67. Needing 193 to win, Victoria lost Ponsford for 17 but Love and Woodfull added 132 runs to swing the game. Love, who had failed to score in the first innings, hit 70 and Woodfull was 94 not out when the game ended.

In the second game against the MCC tourists, Woodfull (six) and Ponsford (62) were overshadowed by their Victorian team mates in a score of six for 617. Love continued his excellent form with 192, while Park (101), Ransford (118) and Liddicut (102) also made centuries.

Woodfull's brief lapse in that match was followed a week later by a resounding innings of 187 for South Melbourne in the last round of District games for 1922–23. Playing at Northcote, this was to remain Woodfull's highest score in District games. The innings, plus hands of 160 by Park and 71 by Pye, enabled Woodfull's team to reach five for 468 although it didn't get the chance to dismiss Northcote. The second day was a washout, not because of rain but due to a 61 cm water main bursting in the early hours of Saturday morning at the western end of the Northcote ground. The break wasn't stopped until 1.45 pm and, while the water didn't reach the pitch, it flooded the grandstand end of the ground. Play was ruled out chiefly because workmen had to fill in a large hole created by the problem.

As neither South Melbourne, which finished eleventh nor St Kilda (fifth) qualified for the finals, the District season finished for the two Bills. Woodfull's 636 runs at an average 63.60 an innings earned him second place in the VCA averages. Ponsford's average of 36.55 contrasted with his first-class average for the season of 154.00.

Strangely enough, Ponsford held the world record for a first-class innings yet had still to score his maiden club century. This singular curiosity was rectified early in the 1923–24 season, when he hit 113 against South Melbourne the day after his 23rd birthday. The break could have come the previous week when Ponsford was 50 not out at Collingwood after the opening day's play, but rain prevented play on the second Saturday.

Apart from Ponsford's first hundred for St Kilda, a sound rather than spectacular knock covering three hours and responsible for exactly half his side's total, the match against South Melbourne was also notable in that Woodfull carried his bat. South batsmen generally struggled against the St Kilda bowling, but Woodfull stood firm for 145 minutes, making 66 not out in a total of 157.

By the following Saturday, when Ponsford made 80 against Richmond and shared a first-wicket stand worth 170 with Bert Cohen (90), Melbourne was in the grip of a police strike. Simmering discontent among police officers had come to a head the previous day when there was a mass walkout of police. The situation was extremely serious on the Saturday when mobs looted city shops, and a special constabulary was formed to restore order. The 'specials' policed the city and suburbs for the next few weeks while a new force was built.

Ponsford and Cohen gave St Kilda another century start, this time at Fitzroy in early December, when they put on 114. Ponsford, who contributed 60 in 108 minutes, had made four half centuries and a century in club matches before Victoria's first game for the season. The match, against Queensland at the MCG, was notable for a first-wicket partnership of 456 between Ponsford and Victorian captain Edgar Mayne. The stand remained a record for any wicket in first-class cricket in Australia until 1986–87.

Queensland, which at that stage had not been admitted to the Sheffield Shield competition, batted first and could make only 162. Mayne and Ponsford took block at 4.10 pm and treated the bowling carefully for the first half hour. The pair then opened out and by stumps had put together a useful 108, of which 'Ponny' had contributed 59 and Mayne 47. At lunch the next day, a Saturday, the pair was still together — Ponsford 127 and Mayne 112 — and Victoria nought for 245. By tea the batsmen had lifted the score to nought for 405, with Ponsford on 231 and Mayne 168.

Ponsford, who had broken away to become the dominant batsman in the big partnership, again showed his extraordinary capacity to concentrate for a long time. It was almost 5 pm when Queensland bowler Ron Oxenham trapped him lbw for 248. Ponsford had batted for 350 minutes and hit 22 fours, his off-driving and pulling bringing many runs. He had given chances at 132 and 170 but otherwise had played very soundly.

Woodfull joined Mayne and the pair took the score to 480 before the latter was out for 209[1]. Mayne closed the innings at two for 538, with Woodfull 46 not out.

Immediately after the Queensland game, Ponsford and Mayne were back at the crease to open for Victoria in the Christmas game against New South Wales at the MCG. For a short time it seemed that the Victorians would repeat their huge partnership, but at 99 New South Wales fast bowler Jack Scott dismissed Ponsford for 45. Mayne went on to make 106 before he, too, fell to Scott whose five for 107 held Victoria to 285. Woodfull hit 23 in what seemed an insufficient total to win the game.

In replying with 268, New South Wales trailed by 17 runs on the first innings. Early interest in Victoria's second innings centred on whether Ponsford could score a century to emulate his feat of a hundred on debut against Tasmania, South Australia and Queensland. He didn't, making 24, but the batting honors for the innings went to the other Bill. Coming in at number three, Woodfull reached 117 before he was bowled by Macartney. His innings enabled Victoria to compile a very sound 412 which left New South Wales a difficult but not impossible target of 430 to win.

The task proved a little too much for New South Wales, despite a hand of 98 from Charlie Kelleway, and the last wicket fell for 386 to give Victoria a 43-run win.

In the space of a fortnight, the MCG was the venue for a third first-class game when Victoria met South Australia in the New Year's clash. Again Victoria asserted itself with strong batting in the second innings. Much of the credit for the home State's eventual 98-run win was due to Ponsford's great form.

Apart from Ponsford, who hit 81, Victoria's batting strength was not evident in the first innings and the modest total of 221 seemed certain to be passed by South Australia. Centuries by both the Richardsons, Arthur and Vic, enabled South Australia to reach 309 although the total could have been higher had they received much support. Liddicut's six for 65 was a fine performance for Victoria.

Woodfull, run out for 14 in the first innings, was bowled for eight by Arthur Richardson in the second, but team mate 'Ponny' found that attack was the best response to the South Australian bowling.

Batting for 213 minutes, he gave Victoria the chance of winning with a knock of 159. His innings, which contained only eight fours, ended when he was caught at the wicket while trying to leg glance.

Needing 270 to win, South Australia was all out for 171; Hartkopf heading the Victorian bowlers with a valuable five for 56.

Having missed out on making a century in his debut against New South Wales, Ponsford hit a century in each innings in the return match in Sydney. After dismissing the home State for 217, Victoria received a setback when it lost Woodfull for nought. Love, who went in as nightwatchman, was out for 31 before Ponsford joined Mayne. In the next 167 minutes 'Ponny' did most of the scoring as the pair added 176 for the third wicket. Before being bowled by Macartney with the first ball of the New South Wales veteran's thirteenth over, Ponsford had hit 110 which included 11 boundaries. Mayne, who carried his bat for 154 not out in a total of 345, was tedious compared with Ponsford.

In its second innings New South Wales improved to total 321, of which Herbie Collins top-scored with 81 and Prahran fast bowler Percy Wallace took five for 99 for Victoria, but it wasn't enough. Victoria needed fewer than 200 runs to win and with Ponsford in such good form the task was well within reach. Ponsford, who opened with Mayne, was 110 not out when a winning score had been achieved at two for 195. Mayne (10) and Woodfull (30) were the two batsmen dismissed.

Victoria completed its Sheffield Shield engagements and clinched the Shield when it beat South Australia in Adelaide by an innings and seven runs. Playing his fifteenth first-class innings, Ponsford was dismissed for a duck for the first time when he was caught off the bowling of Heath.

Despite the loss of a potential century, Victoria was still able to reach a solid 454 of which Hartkopf hit 99, Jack Ellis 94 and Woodfull 62. In reply, South Australia was all out for 191 and 256. Keating took six for 72 in the first innings and Grimmett eight for 86 in the second. Ironically Grimmet transferred to South Australia the following season, played his first game against Victoria and from there won selection in the Australian team.

Following his enormously successful season in first-class games, Ponsford hit another century for St Kilda. Playing North Melbourne, he reached 125 in 208 minutes to contribute to a score of eight for 301. In his only other innings before the finals he made a score of one against Prahran. Apart from a sound 45 against Hawthorn-East Melbourne, Woodfull finished the District season quietly, as did his South Melbourne Club, which ran second last.

St Kilda, by contrast, headed the ladder and convincingly beat Prahran in its semi-final. Allie Lampard made 64 and Ponsford 37 in St Kilda's score of 192, while Don Blackie gave a match-winning performance with seven for 46 in Prahran's total of 104. This brought St Kilda and Northcote together in the final, at the MCG. The big difference between the teams was St Kilda batsman Les Ferguson who made a brilliant 151. Ponsford, who opened the innings, contributed 44 of his side's 372 which easily beat Northcote's 197.

Not surprisingly, Ponsford headed the VCA batting averages with 70.75. He was batting so well that his appearances with St Kilda were obviously going to be very limited in future seasons.

Meanwhile, on Monday March 24, 1924, Ponsford had married. This partnership, like those he shared on the cricket field, was destined to last longer than most. His bride, Vera Neill, was born at Swan Hill, the youngest of a family of six girls and two boys. The family subsequently moved to Melbourne, living at Elsternwick. Vera, who became a milliner, met Bill Ponsford through the Orrong Road Methodist Church Sunday School, where she taught the kindergarten age-group and Bill was the librarian.

In the early 1920s there were still vacant blocks of land in nearby South Caulfield and Glenhuntly and the future Mr and Mrs Ponsford had a home built for them at 32 Laura Street, South Caulfield, which was ready for them to move into after their marriage. Built of tuck-pointed brickwork and featuring diamond-shaped glass in the front windows, the house remained the Ponsfords' home for the next 53 years. The road was unmade at that stage and the fringe of the city barely took in the neighbourhood, but both these aspects were to change.

Fond of watching cricket and going to the theatre, Mrs Ponsford became a devoted wife and mother. In her era it was unusual for a housewife to return to the workforce after raising a family.

NOTES

[1]Mayne, aged 41 and at the end of his career, made his highest first-class score. Born at Jamestown, South Australia, he played with South Australia before World War I and Victoria afterwards. His 14 first-class centuries included six for Victoria. He captained both States and played four Tests. In 1913 he captained an Australian team to the United States and Canada.

His partnership with Ponsford created a record for any wicket in Australian first-class cricket and was the highest by two Australians. It remains a first-wicket record, but the run total was exceeded by South Australians David Hookes and Wayne Phillips who shared an unbeaten fourth-wicket stand of 460 against Tasmania in 1986–87.

TEST SELECTION

HE building of the Capitol Theatre, designed by Walter Burley Griffin, Frank Beaurepaire's continued Olympic Games swimming success and Bill Ponsford's Test selection were all reasons for Melburnians to feel proud at the end of 1924. The last event became an even bigger thrill for cricket devotees when Ponsford hit a century in each of his first two Tests[1] to signal that he could handle the world's best bowling just as well as that in Australia.

In the month leading up to the initial first-class game of the season, both Ponsford and Woodfull made a quiet start with their respective clubs. Woodfull and his brother Balfour ('Jack') had switched from South Melbourne to Carlton[2], while St Kilda had gained 'Hammy' Love from Carlton and Fred Yeomans from Northcote. Melbourne secured a fine recruit in former New South Wales batsman and change bowler, Hunter Hendry.

The Mayor of St Kilda, Cr J.B. Levi, unfurled St Kilda's 1923–24 pennant before the opening game of the new season, against Collingwood. Ponsford followed by batting steadily for an hour, although he had to survive a chance before scoring. He eventually made 43. Woodfull was 21 not out in his game, although rain all but ruined the second day's play. Neither player excelled in the second round and then they were off to Adelaide to play South Australia.

Victoria won the game by three wickets despite trailing by 175 runs on the first innings. Set 409 to win, Victoria achieved the difficult target largely because of the batting of Ponsford, Woodfull and Hendry. Ponsford (77) and Woodfull (67) added 109 for the second wicket and Hendry was 109 not out at the finish.

The English tourists, led by Arthur Gilligan, also found Victoria a problem in their second innings. Woodfull and Ponsford, batting down the list, had made only 20 between them in the first innings and Victoria trailed by 11 runs. Needing 252 to win, Mayne and Park opened the State's second innings but Park was bowled by Gilligan for one. Woodfull joined Mayne and the pair put on 120, Mayne hitting 87 and Woodfull 61. Ponsford was not required to bat. The home side won by six wickets.

Mayne and Woodfull scored valuable half centuries in the second innings of the return game against South Australia, at the MCG. Chasing South Australia's first innings total of 288, Victoria opened with Mayne and Ponsford and thanks to the latter built a lead of 69. Ponsford almost carried his bat, being last man out for 166 in an innings lasting 338 minutes and including 12 fours. By contrast he failed to score in the second innings, but a second-wicket stand of 116 between Mayne (68) and Woodfull (55 not out) guided Victoria to an eight-wicket win.

In the first innings 'Ponny' began stodgily, taking more than an hour to score 20. Aware that the crowd was becoming restless, he said to his partner Frank Tarrant between overs, 'They're giving us hell.' Tarrant, a veteran of many summers, was unconcerned. 'Don't worry Bill, there'll be a different crowd here tomorrow,' he said.

Selection of Ponsford in an Australian XI to play the Englishmen a fortnight before the first Test indicated he was on the verge of joining the Test team. 'Ponny' had to make a good score to continue his advancement, and when he opened the Australian XI innings with Queenslander Leo O'Connor he made the best of the opportunity. In an impressive display, Ponsford hit 81 and the pair put on 121 for the first wicket. The Australians compiled 526, to which the tourists replied with 421, and in the second innings Australia made five for 257. Ponsford wasn't asked to bat. He'd made his contribution.

Ponsford took his Brisbane form into the first Test in Sydney, where Australian skipper Herbie Collins won the toss and opened the innings himself with Warren Bardsley. With the score at 46, Bardsley was out for 21 and Ponsford entered the Test arena for the first time. Already a favourite with the Sydney crowd, he was given a great reception as he walked to the wicket. It wasn't long before Ponsford found that England fast-medium bowler Maurice 'Chub' Tate was difficult to handle. He had not previously faced Tate and was uncomfortable. Collins was aware of Ponsford's problem and helped him by taking strike against Tate as often as possible.

Forever grateful to Collins for his action, Ponsford had no hesitation in naming Tate when asked in 1985 who was the best bowler he had encountered. While Tate worried 'Ponny' in his first spell of bowling, which lasted 19 overs, he didn't remove the young Australian and when he was brought back later in the afternoon he didn't appear as dangerous.

Collins and Ponsford took their partnership to 190 before the former was out for 114. Ponsford, whose driving was strong, reached his century in 206 minutes and added another 10 more runs before being bowled by Gilligan. At stumps on the first day Australia was a very useful three for 282. The next day it was all out for 450, Tate finishing with six for 130.

England replied with 298 after Hobbs (115) and Sutcliffe (59) had opened with a stand of 157. In its second innings Australia reached 452, Johnny Taylor contributing 108 and Arthur Richardson 98. Ponsford, at number four, made 27.

Needing 605 runs to win, Hobbs (57) and Sutcliffe (115) began the impossible task with a partnership of 110. Frank Woolley scored 123 and England did well to make 411 in the fourth innings of the game. Nevertheless, Australia won by 193 runs.

The second Test, in Melbourne, opened with a then world record crowd of 49,413 for a single day's play, beating the 47,152 in Sydney eight days earlier. Collins again won the toss and batted but this time three wickets had fallen for 47 before Ponsford and Taylor became associated in a fourth-wicket stand worth 161. It ended when Taylor was run out by Hobbs for 72.

Ponsford advanced steadily to another hundred, driving Tyldesly 'softly' for a single to reach three figures. His innings was a crisp knock, lasting just under three hours, and enthralled the big crowd.

'The crowd gave him an ovation, and after tumultuous hand-clapping, gave him three cheers,' reported the *Argus*. 'Ponsford had made 100 in his first Test match and shared the honor with several others, but no one else has made 100 in each of his first two games. This boy stands alone as a record-breaker.'

At stumps Australia was four for 300, an admirable recovery, with Ponsford on 128 and Vic Richardson on 39. Already Ponsford was being described as the best Australian batsman since Victor Trumper.

At noon the next day Tate opened the bowling to Richardson who gained a single off the fifth delivery. Then Ponsford received a ball pitched outside the off stump, it turned slightly and Ponsford played it on to his stumps. The Victorian's faultless innings, which

Alfred Crescent State School, North Fitzroy,
where Bill Ponsford was educated.

Fitzroy baseballer Bill Ponsford safely
reaches base during a match against
Richmond in 1922. Ponsford was regarded as
one of the best baseballers in Australia and
was once approached by the New York
Giants.

Bill Ponsford (left) and Karl Schneider during the match against Tasmania in February, 1923 when Ponsford hit a world record score of 429. Schneider, a promising 17-year-old batsman who is wearing his Xavier College blazer, made 55. Tragically Schneider died in September, 1928, soon after his 23rd birthday.

Members of the Victorian XI pose for their picture before a game in 1925. Jack Ryder, later to captain Australia, is standing at the back of the group. In front of him (left) are Bill Woodfull, Jack Ellis, Albert Hartkopf, Bill Ponsford and Roy Park, while those on the right are Percy Wallace, Arthur Liddicut, Edgar Mayne, Carl Willis and Hampden Love.

had occupied 222 minutes and yielded six fours, had ended.

Richardson went on to make 138, which was to remain his sole century in 19 Tests, and some fine lower order support was given by Hartkopf (80), Gregory (44) and Oldfield (39 not out). As a result Australia compiled an even 600, its highest score in any Test at that stage. Previously its best had been 589 against England at the MCG in 1911–12.

England, in reply, began with a massive start of 283 by Hobbs and Sutcliffe. Hobbs, bowled by Mailey in the first over of the fourth day, made 154. Sutcliffe went on to hit 176, but the Englishmen fell away and were all out for 479.

In its second innings, Australia began shakily and lost three wickets for 27. Ponsford, bowled by Tate for four, was in good company as Tate also took the other two wickets. Collins and Taylor consolidated but Collins was bowled by J.W. Hearne for 30 and Australia was four for 106. Taylor, who made 90, held the batting together but when he was out the score was seven for 168. With a lead of 289 and three wickets in hand, Australia needed another 40 or 50 to secure its advantage. Oldfield (39) and Gregory (36 not out) provided this and the innings reached 250.

England, needing 372 to win, lost Hobbs for 22 when Mailey bowled him but Sutcliffe kept his country in the race by making his second century for the match. On January 8, 1925 — the seventh day of the Test — Sutcliffe added 13 before he was out for 127 and England collapsed from six for 259 to be all out for 290, giving Australia an 81-run win.

Despite the brilliance of Tate, who had taken 20 wickets in the opening two Tests, Australia had a 2–0 lead and seemed assured of holding the Ashes. This was achieved after the third Test, in Adelaide, but only after Australia had withstood a gallant fightback by England.

Collins won the toss for the third time and opened the innings with himself and Arthur Richardson. Three wickets fell for only 22 before Ponsford, batting at number five, joined Richardson to steady a shaky innings. The pair brought up the century, but soon after Ponsford was caught at the wicket for 31 and Richardson left for 69. Victorian Jack Ryder, aided by Tommy Andrews and Oldfield, not only rescued the Australian side but put it in a winning position. Ryder batted for six and a half hours to score 201 not out, Andrews hit 72 and Oldfield 47 in a handsome total of 489.

England replied with 365, of which Hobbs made 119 and Elias 'Patsy' Hendren 92. Australia in its second innings again began with

Collins and A. Richardson, but promoted Ryder to number three. Ryder made 88 to become the first player to score a double century and a half century in a Test. Ponsford, who remained at number five, provided a useful 43 but he and 'The King' stood out from the other batsmen and Australia had to be content with 250.

Australia had begun the fifth day of the match 335 runs ahead with seven wickets in hand, including those of Ryder and Ponsford, but lost seven for 39 on a gluepot pitch that was capably exploited by Woolley and Roy Kilner. This left England the daunting task of scoring 375 to win on a troublesome pitch.

Naturally the old firm of Hobbs and Sutcliffe could be expected to give a sound start. Hobbs was first out for 27 with the total 63, but Sutcliffe endured the rest of the day, losing Woolley and Hendren along the way.

On the sixth day the great Yorkshire opener was out for 59, leaving England four wickets down for 155, but half centuries by 'Dodger' Whysall and Chapman kept the visitors in the game. At four for 244 England was in with a chance, but the loss of two wickets for the addition of 10 runs swung the game back in Australia's favour. Kilner and Tate helped lift the total to eight for 312, but with only 'Tich' Freeman and Herbert Strudwick to partner Gilligan, 63 runs seemed an almost impossible target for a victory.

Gilligan and Freeman took advantage of a tiring attack, gained in confidence as they went along and more than halved the deficit. Then rain stopped play, possibly saving Australia from defeat or perhaps merely prolonging the inevitable. The upshot was that the game went into the seventh day with England needing 27 to win and two wickets standing.

Gilligan spent a sleepless sixth night. So too did Mailey but under different circumstances. He went out for the night, had a good time and finished up at the flat in which Collins was staying. As dawn broke across Adelaide, the pair looked out the window to the distant Adelaide Oval. Mailey pondered on the attack Collins would open with later in the day and asked if it would be Gregory and Charlie Kelleway. 'No,' said Collins, 'Gregory and you. It's to be all duck, or nothing for dinner.'[3]

Considering that Mailey often paid many runs for his wickets, Collins was obviously gambling[4] to the extreme. Mailey's night out seemed unwise, but in the end it didn't matter.

When play resumed it was Gregory who caused an anxious moment, giving away four byes with an erratic delivery. England needed only 23 to win. The next ball was a yorker, but Freeman survived to hit a two later in the over. Two singles off Mailey came during the next over and then came the break. With 18 needed to win, Gilligan drove Gregory uppishly and was caught by Vic Richardson. Strudwick joined Freeman and the pair pruned six runs off the target before Mailey began the sixth over of the day.

Freeman let the first delivery pass, the next he defended but was beaten by the break and Oldfield stretched to the right and held the catch. Australia had won by 11 runs. It was its eighth consecutive Test win against England.

The following day Victoria began a Shield match against New South Wales in Sydney. Ponsford didn't play — he wouldn't have had time to get there from Adelaide by train — but Woodfull excelled himself with knocks of 81 and 120 not out to help Victoria to a seven-wicket win. The match was notable in that two New South Wales batsmen — Harry Rock (235) and Alan Kippax (212 not out) — scored a double century in their side's first innings total of 614, yet their side was still beaten.

Victoria replied with 502, Woodfull playing a slow hand for 81 before being run out and Liddicut and Willis each hitting a century. New South Wales managed only 152 in the face of some skilful bowling by Hartkopf and Hendry in its second innings, although Rock (51) and Kippax (41) were again prominent. Woodfull's second innings century, aided by 85 from Hendry, steered Victoria to a comfortable win.

No sooner had that game finished than players were bound for Melbourne to begin the return game the next day. The VCA had wanted to postpone the start by a day, but the New South Wales Cricket Association (NSWCA) executive would not agree. Woodfull didn't play but Ponsford came into the team and top-scored in both Victoria's innings, making 80 and 38. Despite half centuries from Collins and Bardsley, New South Wales trailed Victoria's first innings 295 by 17. Victoria reached only 155 in its second knock and New South Wales won by three wickets, inflicting Victoria's sole defeat for the season.

In a busy schedule, Victoria began its second game against the English tourists at the MCG only three days after the second New South Wales fixture, which itself had been completed ahead of time. Ponsford didn't play but Woodfull returned to the side, which was soundly beaten by the visitors.

Johnny Douglas captained the MCC in the absence of Gilligan who was injured. Sutcliffe (88), Hearne (193) and Whysall (89) enabled their side to score 500, despite a hat-trick by Bert Ironmonger, which completed the innings. Tate, Strudwick and Howell were the three batsmen to fall in successive deliveries.

Apart from Woodfull (60) and Ransford (62), Victoria's batsmen struggled and with only 179 to show for their efforts were asked to follow on. Caught on a 'sticky', the second innings on the uncovered pitch was a complete disaster. Woodfull was out for two and Victoria at one stage sank to six for 14 before being all out for 50. Kilner, who took five wickets for 18, and Hearne (five for 30) were the only bowlers used.

Australia went into the fourth Test at the MCG with a 3–0 lead and Ponsford had already made 343 runs at an average of 57.16. The match, which started on Friday February 13, brought a change in fortune for England, which had not beaten Australia in a Test since 1912.

Hobbs and Sutcliffe obliged their country with a start of 126, but the partnership could have been broken much earlier. Aware that the English pair would be hard to shift, Collins asked fast bowler Jack Gregory to bowl the fourth ball of a certain over a little short in the hope that Sutcliffe would be tempted to hook. The idea was that Ponsford, the fine leg fieldsman to Gregory's bowling, would walk some 40 metres squarer and then move in 15 metres to be somewhere around backward square-leg. The plan began perfectly 'Ponny' went for a walk, Gregory bowled a short one on the leg side and Sutcliffe hooked uppishly in Ponsford's direction. What a clever tactician Collins had proved. Alas, one matter went awry. Ponsford spilled the chance and a further 99 runs were added before the first wicket fell. More than once Ponsford apologised to Collins for the slip, which was not characteristic of his normally sound fielding.

Eventually Hobbs was out for 66, but Sutcliffe soldiered on and made 143. After such a fine start it was little wonder that the English batsmen rallied and finished with a commanding total of 548. Australia replied with barely half that score, being all out for 269. Ponsford, who batted at number five, gave a difficult chance off Tate to Kilner before he had scored but then batted steadily for three-quarters of an hour to make 21. Taylor top-scored with 86.

Forced to follow on, Australia lost Collins and Bardsley with only five runs scored. Gregory (45), Ryder (38), Taylor (68) and Kelleway (42) battled hard to build a big score but it wasn't enough and the final total of 250 meant England had won by an innings and 29 runs. Ponsford, batting at number eight, made 19 in an uncertain knock before being bowled by Tate whose five for 75 gave him 29 wickets for the series.

Australia made a winning move for the fifth and final Test, in Sydney, by including Grimmett for his first Test. His figures of five for 45 and six for 37 underlined the concern he caused the Englishmen and set up Australia's 307-run win. Ponsford, too, played a major part by top-scoring with 80 in Australia's first innings.

Collins won the toss for the fourth time in the series and batted. In a hand highlighted by forceful driving and bright stroke-making on the leg side, 'Ponny' made his runs in 140 minutes. According to the *Argus* there were two distinct phases to Ponsford's innings. In the early stage he looked like getting out at any moment but later, when he was chasing runs, he looked secure.

The sixth-wicket stand of 105 between Ponsford and Kippax saved the side from collapse, but even 'Ponny' couldn't lift the score beyond a mediocre seven for 239 at stumps on the first day. Dismissed for 295, Australia found itself in a relatively strong position when England lost Hobbs, Sutcliffe, Sandham and Hendren for a combined total of 36 and then struggled against Grimmett who took five of the last six wickets.

All out for 167, England ran out Ponsford for five in Australia's second innings, but a hand of 80 by Tommy Andrews and an eighth-wicket stand of 116 between Kelleway and Oldfield enabled the home side to reach 325. Kelleway hit 73 and Oldfield was unbeaten on 65.

Needing 454 to win, England's task became all but impossible when Gregory bowled Sutcliffe for a duck. Then Grimmett took over and England fared even worse than it had in the first innings, to be all out for 146.

Grimmett's 11 wickets at a cost of 7.45 runs per wicket won him the Australian bowling average. Ryder headed the Australian batting with 72.6, while Ponsford was fourth with 46.8. England openers Sutcliffe — 734 runs at 81.55 — and Hobbs — 573 runs at 63.66 — enjoyed a great series, as did Tate who finished with 38 wickets.

Meanwhile, a Victorian team comprising Mayne, Woodfull, Ransford, Willis, Liddicut, Wallace, H. Austin, E. Austen, Ellis, Ebeling, Hartkopf and Millar had begun a short tour of New Zealand which included two unofficial Tests. Woodfull, with only 18 first-class games behind him, batted with the aplomb of a veteran. In his three innings in the 'Tests' he remained not out on each occasion for an aggregate of 310 runs. In all first-class games he batted nine times, averaging a hefty 176.50 by virtue of five uncompleted innings. His 706 runs included a double century, two centuries and three half centuries.

Woodfull's double century was scored against Canterbury in Christchurch at a stage when Victoria needed some heavy scoring to avoid defeat. The tourists had trailed Canterbury by almost 200 runs on the first innings and when they batted a second time 'Woody' steered them to seven for 448 with a hand of 212 not out. Victoria wasn't so fortunate against Wellington. Needing 237 in its second innings to win, Woodfull provided 56 but the visitors were still 19 runs behind when they lost their last wicket.

Woodfull's one poor game, against Auckland when he was dismissed for four, didn't affect the final result, as Ransford hit an unbeaten 106, Harold Austin hit 87 and E. Austen made 82 in a total of 434. The match was drawn.

Victoria won the first unofficial Test, in Wellington, by six wickets. This was due largely to the batting of Woodfull and to Ransford's bowling. Victoria replied to New Zealand's first innings of 226 with 336, to which Woodfull contributed 110 not out, and Ransford restricted the New Zealand second innings to 251 with the excellent figures of six for 38. Requiring 142 to win, the tourists hit four for 147 with Woodfull 50 not out.

The second 'Test', in Christchurch, was drawn. Prahran paceman Percy Wallace helped Victoria to a good start with a haul of five for 65 in a total of only 237. Victoria appeared in danger of not reaching that figure when it lost its fourth wicket for 114, but Ransford joined Woodfull and the pair enjoyed an unbroken fifth-wicket stand of 235 before Mayne closed the innings at four for 349. Woodfull was 150 not out and Ransford 100 not out. New Zealand scored five for 74 in its second innings.

Apart from enjoying his cricket in New Zealand, Woodfull was most impressed with the physical beauty of the land. In later years he advised his children 'never go to Switzerland until you've seen New Zealand'.

While Woodfull was enhancing his chances of Test selection in England in 1926, Ponsford completed a very successful 1924–25 season by helping St Kilda win the VCA premiership. St Kilda, a powerful side even without Ponsford, headed the ladder with 27 points from nine wins and a draw in its 10 games for the season. Hawthorn-East Melbourne and Prahran, the second and third teams, scored 16 points while fourth-placed Richmond had 15. Carlton was sixth with 13 points.

In its semi-final against Prahran, St Kilda hit 262 to which its opponents replied with 114 and five for 195. Ponsford was the batting star with 108 and Blackie's first innings return of five for 54 wrecked

Prahran's chances of success.

St Kilda performed even better in the final against Richmond, winning by an innings and 153 runs. Ponsford made 67 out of a total of 321, to which most of the St Kilda players contributed, and Blackie and Ironmonger took all 20 Richmond wickets. Blackie took 11 of these, and Richmond folded first for 75 and then for 93.

Bill Woodfull's capacity as a leader was acknowledged by his club, Carlton, which made him captain in 1925–26. He began the new season with a neat, sound innings of 61 in 114 minutes against Hawthorn-East Melbourne and followed with 83 against Richmond in the next game. Most of his runs in the latter innings were scored on the on-side.

Ponsford also showed top form early in the season, hitting a brisk 60 against South Melbourne in conditions more favourable to bowlers and 154 in only three hours against Essendon. His batting against Essendon was faultless before he reached 100 and when he did give chances at 130 and 140 it was because he was chasing the bowling. Ponsford, who put on 93 with Cohen for the first wicket, hit 12 fours and one six.

Both Ponsford and Woodfull appeared for Victoria against Western Australia at Fitzroy. It was the first time Western Australia had played in Melbourne since 1912 and only its eighth game against Victoria. Given the chance to show his qualities as an opener Ponsford accepted by reeling off a swift century[5]. He and Mayne began the innings late in the day after Ironmonger's seven for 30 had restricted Western Australia to 151. Only 59 minutes had lapsed before Mayne and Ponsford posted a century stand and by stumps 'Ponny' had reached 103 in 102 minutes. The next day, after giving an easy chance at 111, he took his score to 158 in 170 minutes with 12 fours.

Ponsford had shared an opening partnership of 140 with Mayne, and helped add 126 for the second wicket with Love, who eventually reached 103. Woodfull, batting down the list because of a bruised finger, made 28 in Victoria's total of 536. West Australian bowler Merv Inverarity toiled away admirably to finish with six for 162. In its second innings the West again disappointed, compiling only 103.

Victoria's defence of the Sheffield Shield, which it had held for two years, received a setback when it visited Adelaide for its first game of the season. Although it led by 105 runs on the first innings, Victoria couldn't handle a deteriorating pitch when it batted a second time and its total of 182 left South Australia the winner by 123 runs. Ponsford managed only six in the first innings and made an uncomfortable 19 in the second. Woodfull made 13 and 44, his second innings earning praise as Victoria battled to avert defeat.

Early in December 1925, Ponsford and Woodfull played in an Australian XI against The Rest in Sydney. This was a Test trial under first-class conditions. Obviously good performances were vital to ensure a place in the team to tour England the following year.

The Rest began the game with 380, with Kelleway left on 99 not out. Collins opened the Australian XI innings with Ponsford. It was a prime chance for 'Ponny' to prove that his forte was opening the innings rather than coming in at number four or lower. With 17 runs to his name he seemed set to make the point, but then Kelleway bowled him. Woodfull was run out for 11 and wickets fell regularly, but Collins kept his wicket intact. The Australian XI skipper eventually made 102 in a total of 226.

Batting a second time, The Rest was all out for 298 and at stumps on the third day Australia was none for 25 with Ponsford and Woodfull at the crease. It was the first time the pair had opened. Woodfull batted soundly for 42, but Ponsford was out for 10. Woodfull was one of four top-order batsmen dismissed by Grimmett who finished with five for 91, despite conceding 18 off an over to Gregory. Although Gregory hit 100 and Collins 81, the Australian XI innings finished at 296 to give victory to The Rest by 156 runs.

Neither Ponsford nor Woodfull played against New Zealand at the MCG before Christmas. 'Stork' Hendry dominated the drawn game and the Victorian score of seven for 592 (dec.) with an unbeaten 325.

In the Christmas match against New South Wales at the MCG, Mayne and Woodfull opened the Victorian innings and Ponsford batted at the fall of the third wicket. Both hit a half century and 'Hammy' Love top-scored with 115 in a total of 413. The visitors replied with 705 and won the game by an innings when Victoria collapsed for 130 in its second innings. Woodfull made 13 and Ponsford, coming in at number eight, was 25 not out when the game finished.

At this point 12 players were named to tour England — the remaining four were to be selected later — and Ponsford was among those chosen. Woodfull wasn't one of the original 12, but he probably clinched a place with a splendid double in the New Year game against South Australia at the MCG, a match Ponsford missed.

Despite 97 from Woodfull, Victoria's batting problems continued and its total of 232 was easily surpassed by South Australia. Colin Alexander, a 19-year-old making his Shield debut, hit 133 to help the visitors to a 230-run lead on the first innings. Woodfull's patient batting, for which he was becoming renowned, enabled Victoria to get back into the game in its second innings. For six and three-quarter hours he defied the South Australian bowling, steadily accumulating singles and twos with a four almost every half hour. When he reached 200 he was greeted by a great outburst of applause from the crowd, followed by three cheers. The South Australian players also gathered around him to offer their congratulations.

Ryder, deputising for Mayne as Victoria's captain, hit 95 and helped 'Woody' add 233 for the fourth wicket. Woodfull's final score of 236 gave him a match total of 333 and enabled Victoria to compile 604 in its second innings.

The *Argus* acknowledged Woodfull's batting, saying: 'If courage, determination and the power to rise above circumstances are essentials in a Test match player, Woodfull possesses them to a marked degree.

'Of all his peformances, none perhaps is more valuable from the point of view of a prospective batsman for England than his 60 against the MCC on a bowler's wicket last February. In that innings he proved himself just the man for English wickets.

'The innings which Woodfull played yesterday, following his 97 in the first innings and his 53 against New South Wales, shows that he is in tip-top form, and that he is improving with every innings. He went in with Victoria well behind. He had to play excellent bowling, for Grimmett has not bowled better than he did yesterday morning. At one stage he bowled seven overs for 13 runs and two wickets, and it was Woodfull who took the edge off his bowling. The innings was resourceful, and it was with his back to the wall that he played his best.'

Needing 375 to win, South Australia lost three wickets for 38 before rain interrupted play for two days. When the game resumed the pitch gave the batting side no chance as Hendry showed with six for 30. South Australia was all out for 87, giving Victoria a remarkable win by 287 runs.

Ponsford was at his brilliant best in the return game against New South Wales in Sydney. He followed a first innings gem of 79 with an entertaining 138 in the second visit to the crease. More than half Victoria's runs in the second innings were made during a fourth-wicket partnership of 178 between the two Bills. Woodfull's yield for the game was 15 in the first innings and 126 in the second.

If Woodfull had won himself a trip to England with his double century against South Australia, New South Wales batsman Alan Kippax should have done so in his match against Victoria. After dismissing Victoria for 230, New South Wales set about making a huge score with Collins hitting 143 and Kippax 271 not out. Kippax, who batted for 432 minutes and hit 30 fours, shared century stands with Kelleway and Oldfield and was chiefly responsible for New South Wales reaching 708.

The batting of Ponsford and Woodfull highlighted Victoria's second innings. While they were together Woodfull scored 85 to Ponsford's 92 and overall Woodfull scored slightly faster with 126 in 168 minutes to Ponsford's 138 in 195 minutes. Ponsford displayed flair all around the wicket, while Woodfull's innings was considered his best in Sydney to that stage. Both players were bowled by Sam Everett, a pace bowler.

At the end of January 1926, Ponsford had scored 520 runs in first-class games that season, giving him an average of 65.00. Woodfull had hit 678 runs at 61.63 and Kippax 585 at 83.57. The extra places in the team for England were given to South Australian all-rounder Arthur Richardson, Woodfull, Victorian wicketkeeper Jack Ellis and Everett. The omission of Kippax still evokes comment from older cricket enthusiasts.

Woodfull celebrated his selection with a hand of 135 for Carlton against Melbourne in his next club game. Batting only 192 minutes against an attack featuring Ebeling, Hendry and Armstrong, he did not give a chance until past his century. His sound innings contained only five fours.

Ponsford, too, returned to his club in great style and after he and Cohen had put on 81 for the first wicket, he boosted his own score to 96. Made in 131 minutes with 11 fours, the score was highlighted by straight driving and some masterly pulling and glancing.

There was no time for further club games for Ponsford and Woodfull, the pair had both shortly to leave on the English tour. Despite Ponsford's absence St Kilda easily beat Hawthorn-East Melbourne in the VCA final to win its third consecutive flag. Blackie and Iron-monger were the only bowlers used by St Kilda.

NOTES

[1]This feat wasn't emulated by an Australian batsman until Doug Walters hit a century in each of his first two Tests against England in 1965–66.

[2]The family had shifted to 82 Blyth Street, Brunswick.

[3]*Great Cricket Matches*, edited by E.H. Buchanan.

[4]Collins, often known as 'Lucky' or 'Horseshoe', was a card player, heavy punter and later a registered bookmaker.

[5]Ponsford had earlier made a century on debut against Tasmania, South Australia and Queensland, and in his second game against New South Wales had hit a century in each innings. He also hit a century on his debut for Australia against England.

ON ENGLISH SOIL

AUSTRALIA had had phenomenal success in Test cricket against England and South Africa after World War I. This run ended on the 1926 tour of England[1]. Only one of the five Tests was finished, the fifth, and it resulted in a resounding win to England.

Ponsford at 25 and Woodfull at 28 were among the youngest members of a very experienced Australian XI. Bardsley, at 43, was the veteran of the team, while skipper Collins was 37. Mailey, Macartney, Ryder, Andrews and Arthur Richardson were also on the wrong side of 35. Perhaps there wasn't enough young blood in the team. Certainly the non-selection of Kippax was a blunder, especially when only three batsmen — Macartney, Bardsley and Woodfull — averaged more than 31 in Tests. However if the batting left much to be desired, the bowling was a rank failure. No bowler averaged less than 30 runs per wicket and Mailey, the highest wicket-taker with 14, had to pay 42 runs for each dismissal.

The arrival of Ponsford and Woodfull, particularly the former, was eagerly awaited by English cricket enthusiasts. Ponsford's development had been followed with great interest since his monumental 429; the cricket world was keen to see how he adapted to English conditions. Not surprisingly, Woodfull handled the bowlers and pitches with greater skill. His short back lift and straight bat in playing defensively were more in tune with the average English opening batsman than the technique used by Australians. Ponsford, who hit only 37 runs in the two Tests he played, wasn't helped by an enforced break due to tonsilitis a third of the way through the tour.

Woodfull did so well that the English press predicted that he would captain Australia one day. Apart from two centuries in six Test innings, he hit 1672 runs on the tour and was named by *Wisden* as one of its five cricketers of 1927.

In those days cricket tours of England took up more than half the year, starting at the end of February with a series of first-class games in Australia and finishing with the arrival home in November. Woodfull, after four years teaching at Williamstown High School, was appointed to Frankston High School for 1926 but he had to take leave of absence from February to November in order to make the tour of England. On returning from the tour he began teaching at Melbourne High School where he was to stay until posted to Bendigo High School in 1941.

Before the 1926 Australian tourists sailed for London they played first-class games in Launceston, Hobart and Perth. In each case the tourists beat the State by an innings. Woodfull and Ponsford grossed almost 400 runs, while veterans Bardsley and Macartney showed they still had the knack of scoring centuries. In Launceston Woodfull played an unusually vigorous innings that yielded 148, including 15 fours, and Ponsford made 62. Mailey was the best of the bowlers with returns of five for 46 and five for 69.

The second game against Tasmania provided a similar result, except that Macartney (163 not out) and Bardsley (124) were the batting stars. Woodfull, at number four, was out for 17.

The party then returned to Melbourne to catch a train to Perth and, before boarding the *Otranto* to sail to England, again displayed its batting strength. Woodfull was run out without scoring, but Ponsford hit 102 and Johnny Taylor 148.

After the long sea voyage the players were given a second-class game against the Minor Counties to find their land legs. Neither Ponsford (12) nor Woodfull (19) got going, but the former made a bright debut by hitting 56 in the opening first-class fixture at Leicester. Jack Gregory, who was unbeaten on 120, was the only player to do better in an Australian total of 336.

Woodfull did not play at Leicester, but was included for the next game against Essex at Leyton where he signalled his English first-class debut with 201. Woodfull opened with Collins, but the Australian skipper was bowled for nought off the second ball. Undaunted, Woodfull and Macartney added 270 for the second wicket before 'the Governor General'[1] left for 148. Woodfull, meanwhile, reached his century in 130 minutes and in a chanceless innings occupying only four hours carried his score to 201. At that stage he went down the pitch for a big hit, missed and was bowled. His innings had included 14 fours and 81 singles.

Any thoughts that the school master from the Antipodes might not be able to repeat that form were dispelled in the next match, against Surrey at The Oval, when Woodfull again top-scored with a hand of 118 in a total of nine for 395 (dec.). Surrey replied with 265 and the match, like the previous two, was drawn.

Ponsford was included and Woodfull rested for the game against Hampshire at Southampton, in which the bowling of Mailey set up the tourists' first win — by 10 wickets — but there was still a long way to go until the first Test. Both the Bills were chosen to play against the MCC at Lord's. Woodfull failed to score, but Ponsford celebrated his debut at the home of cricket with an unbeaten 110. An unfinished last-wicket partnership of 119 with Arthur Richardson (50) enabled him to complete the century, which he reached in 210 minutes. In reply to the Australian score of nine for 383 (dec.) the MCC made 199 and five for 83 to draw the match.

Although he saved the Australians from trailing against Cambridge University with an unbeaten 98 in a score of 235, Woodfull did not bat at his best. Both he and Ponsford, who made 11, were being juggled around the batting order. From batting at number five against Cambridge Woodfull was given an opening position with Bardsley against Oxford University in the next game. Woodfull made 21 and his team-mates combined to make 300, which was enough to bring an innings win.

The team then visited Bristol to play South of England. Chasing a modest 211, the Australians hit six for 328 which included a fourth-wicket stand of 54 between opener Woodfull (69) and Ponsford (23) who batted at number five. Obviously the decision to open with Woodfull was paying dividends, he was running into form worthy of Test selection, whereas the use of Ponsford down the list was not bringing out the best in him.

Another workout at Lord's followed, this time against Middlesex, and the tourists put together a solid 489 of which Andrews hit 164 and Collins 99. Woodfull made only three, but in a second innings total of five for 239 he hit 100 in 150 minutes. His crisp knock contained nine fours, the last raising his century, and 43 singles.

Both the Bills disappointed in the next two games, against North of England and Yorkshire, but obviously Woodfull had done enough to earn his first Test cap. Ponsford had not played as well as expected, averaging only 34. Fate helped the selectors make up their minds as an attack of tonsilitis put him out of action. Even for the fit and in-form Woodfull, however, the match was a non-event. England captain Arthur Carr, using an Australian penny, won the toss and batted, but rain stopped play for the day with England no wicket for 32. Rain continued for the next two days and play was abandoned.

The second Yorkshire game was also severely curtailed by rain, but there was enough time for Mailey to spin the tourists to an innings win against Lancashire. Woodfull was run out for one and hit 53 not out against Derbyshire in the game preceding the second Test, at Lord's.

Collins won the toss and batted, opening the innings with Bardsley and himself. Woodfull came in at number four and scored 13 before being caught at the wicket off fast bowler Fred Root. Root had taken seven for 42 for North of England several weeks earlier, when the Australians made a lowly total of 105. A powerful batting line-up, featuring Ryder at number nine, reached 383, with Bardsley carrying his bat for 193 not out. Young Nottinghamshire bowler Harold Larwood, making his Test debut, dismissed Macartney and Gregory at a cost of 99 runs.

During this match English amateurs and professionals entered the arena through the same gate for the first time at Lord's, and the old firm of Hobbs and Sutcliffe gave England a start of 182 to which Hendren added an unbeaten 127. Carr declared at three for 475 and Australia was five for 194 in its second innings — Woodfull was yet to score — when time ran out.

By this stage Ponsford was well again and he was used at number eight against Northamptonshire with a view to regaining touch. His innings of 32 was a bright one, especially on the off-side. Bardsley followed up his Test century with 112 and spinners Mailey and Grimmett proved too good for the county batsmen who were all out for 125 in both innings.

The tourists gained another innings win against Nottinghamshire, Mailey's contribution being seven for 110 and eight for 83. Woodfull, who took 40 minutes to reach double figures, was 102 not out when his team was all out for 468. Andrews (91), Bardsley (87) and Macartney (81) also scored heavily, while 'Loll' Larwood bowled well for his three for 88 despite the supremacy of the batsmen.

A brisk 33 in 35 minutes and 30 not out against Worcestershire failed to win Ponsford a place in the third Test at Leeds. Collins didn't play because of neuritis and Grimmett was included to strengthen the bowling. Bardsley became captain and Woodfull was promoted to open the batting with him. Carr won the toss and sent Australia in to bat.

Bardsley, who had endured the entire first innings of the previous Test, was out first ball when he snicked Tate to Sutcliffe at slip. Macartney gave a hard chance but treated the bad start with contempt rather than concern and in only 79 minutes he and Woodfull had posted 100 runs, of which 'the Governor-General' had contributed 83. After 103 minutes Macartney reached his own century and at lunch was 112. Woodfull, playing a lesser but nevertheless valuable role, was 40[3].

After the break Woodfull accelerated his scoring and the pair took the stand to 235 before Macartney was caught at mid-off by Hendren off Yorkshireman George Macaulay for 151, made in only 175 minutes with 21 boundaries. Woodfull batted for the rest of the day, reaching his century in 220 minutes, and when stumps were drawn early because of rain he was 134 not out in a total of three for 366. On resuming the next day he added seven before being bowled by Tate for 141, his innings taking five hours and comprising 12 fours, three threes, 14 twos and 56 singles. The batting of Macartney and Woodfull, followed by 100 from Richardson, allowed Australia to reach a commanding 494.

In reply, England tumbled from a sound score of one for 104 to eight for 182 when Macaulay joined fellow paceman George Geary. Apart from dismissing Macartney, Macaulay had failed with the ball by taking one for 123 off 32 overs. As a tailender he excelled himself with the bat, hitting a timely 76 and helping add an invaluable 108 for the ninth wicket. England, all out for 294, followed on but a stand of 156 by Hobbs and Sutcliffe led to a second innings score of three for 254 which drew the game.

The only first-class game played by the Australians between the third and fourth Tests was at Liverpool where former Victorian and Test fast bowler Ted McDonald was playing with Lancashire. Despite a return of five for 135 by McDonald, the Australian batsmen compiled six for 468 (dec.) after Woodfull (65) and Bardsley (155) had put on 119 for the first wicket. Ponsford made 50 and Andrews 95. Ponsford, who followed with a century in a second-class game against West of Scotland, was included in the fourth Test team at the expense of Taylor. Collins again was omitted.

Australia batted first but rain on the opening day forced abandonment when the score stood at no wicket for six. On resumption, Woodfull and Bardsley took the score to 29 before the latter was out for 15. Woodfull and Macartney then became associated in another huge second-wicket stand, this time adding 192. Although not as brilliant as he was at Leeds, Macartney dashed to another century before being bowled by Fred Root for 109. Woodfull did not play a poor stroke until 117 when he was caught by Hendren at silly leg. His innings had taken 260 minutes and comprised six fours, five threes, 16 twos and 46 singles.

Once Woodfull was out, Australia struggled to build on its fine start. Andrews, Richardson and Ryder fell cheaply and Ponsford's 23 was below expectations. Gregory made 34 to help the tourists to 335, which the home team would have passed had time permitted. When the third and final day's play ended, England was five for 305 with Hendren and Roy Kilner at the crease. With so much time available for county games, it seemed strange that five days could not be set aside for Tests.

Woodfull's excellent form was once more displayed when the tourists visited The Oval for their second game against Surrey. Opening the innings he hit 156, taking 270 minutes and including 11 fours. Ponsford put his Test place in jeopardy by making only one run, but more than atoned in the next two fixtures.

Playing Glamorgan at Swansea, 'Ponny' batted so well he carried his bat for 143 not out in a total of only 283. Batting for 225 minutes he cracked 17 fours and was generously applauded by the crowd for his effort. Woodfull, who batted down the list for eight, was 49 not out in the second innings. Ponsford made 24.

On to Birmingham and Ponsford was again in fine touch against Warwickshire. With Woodfull, who hit 51, he helped the Australians to a start of 117 and then took his own score to 144. Powerful drives, cuts and the occasional leg glance highlighted his 225 minutes at the crease, which included 15 fours. Australia totalled 464.

The fifth Test, at The Oval, was regarded by English observers as one of the great Tests. England, in winning by 289 runs, regained the Ashes which Australia had won so decisively in 1920–21. Despite the overwhelming margin at the finish, England had trailed on the first innings but some magnificent batting by Hobbs and Sutcliffe turned the game. With the Ashes at stake the Test was declared timeless, although four days was, in the end, sufficient time to get a result.

Collins returned to lead Australia while England dropped Carr in favour of Percy Chapman. In another daring but winning move, veteran Wilfred Rhodes was recalled at 48. The selectors reasoned that Rhodes, who had played his first Test way back in 1899, was still playing soundly for Yorkshire and could prove valuable with the ball.

Chapman won the toss and batted. The redoubtable Hobbs and

Bowlers knew they had a difficult task breaking this partnership. Bill Woodfull (left) and Bill Ponsford on their way to the wicket during a Test match.

Four of the sporting world's all-time greats combine in Paris for an unusual picture. American tennis champion Helen Wills, who won Wimbledon eight times, chats to Woodfull (left), Ponsford and Clarrie Grimmett.

The fathers of the great opening pair, Bill Ponsford (sen.) and Rev. Thomas Woodfull, watching their sons during a match at the Melbourne Cricket Ground.

The signatures of the 1926 Australian tourists alongside a photograph of the ship, *H.M.S. Otranto*, on which they sailed to England. Among the signatures, Tommy Andrews appears twice.

Sutcliffe were untroubled in taking the score to 53 until the former played over a full-pitched delivery from Mailey and was bowled for 37. Mailey also bowled Frank Woolley (18) and Sutcliffe (76) on his way to a haul of six for 138 off 33.5 overs which restricted England to 280. It was Mailey's best bowling of the series.

Woodfull and Bardsley opened the Australian innings, but this was soon broken when the latter was caught at the wicket off Larwood for two. By stumps Australia was in trouble at four for 60, having also lost Macartney for 25, Ponsford for two and Andrews for three. Ponsford was run out by a brilliant piece of fielding by Larwood and Andrews was bowled by Larwood.

In need of a big stand, Woodfull and Collins had put on 30 when play resumed but Woodfull was bowled by Rhodes for 35. Richardson also fell to Rhodes, for 16, and at six for 122 it seemed Australia would trail England. Jack Gregory joined Collins and the pair added 107 in an invaluable seventh-wicket partnership. Gregory hit 10 fours in his 73, overtaking Collins whose 61 took almost four hours. Oldfield and Grimmett also shared a useful stand of 67, lifting Australia's total to 302.

England, 22 in arrears, had an hour left to bat on the second day and Hobbs and Sutcliffe not only kept their wickets but also scored a handy 49. Despite an overnight downpour, which turned the pitch into a batting hazard, the great openers made light of the situation and by lunch had steered England to a commanding 161 without the loss of a wicket. Hobbs was 99. After the interval, he patiently waited and scored the single he needed for his century but in the next over was bowled by Gregory. This was Hobbs' first Test century against Australia on his home ground.

With 172 on which to build a solid score, England's succeeding batsmen could not match the skills of the openers. Not that it mattered, Sutcliffe went on to make 161 before he was bowled by Mailey for the second time in the match. This gave the Sydney spinner 97 wickets in his Test career. He also captured the final two wickets of the innings, but was destined not to play another Test.

England, having reached a secure second innings total of 436, set Australia an imposing 415 for victory. The target was soon beyond the tourists. Woodfull was caught in slips off Larwood before he'd scored and Macartney went the same way for 16. Ponsford could manage only 12, being one of four victims snared by the wily Rhodes. At eight for 87 it seemed Australia would be doing well to reach 100. Thanks to Oldfield, who top-scored with 23, Australia finished with 125 while Rhodes (four for 44) and Larwood (three for 34) consummated the English victory.

In the remaining first-class matches of the tour, Woodfull played one more innings of note when the tourists met North of England at Blackpool. Batting the entire 270 minutes the Australians were at the crease, Woodfull carried his bat for 116 not out in a total of 281.[4]

The English tour marked the end of the Test careers of top New South Wales players Collins, Bardsley, Macartney and Mailey, but one fine replacement had been found in Woodfull. In choosing him as one of its five cricketers of the year, *Wisden* said of him: 'It is not exaggeration to say that Woodfull was probably the most difficult man in the Australian team to bowl out. He had no pretensions to grace or style — indeed, at first sight he gave the impression of being rather clumsy — but as to his ability there can not be two opinions.

'He watched the ball more closely than any of his colleagues, and kept his bat beautifully straight. His action seemed a little laboured by reason of the fact that he never lifted the bat any noticeable distance from the ground, but, blessed with strong forearms, he could drive with great power.'

Wisden's other four players were Australian wicketkeeper Bert Oldfield, Leicester medium-pace bowler George Geary, Larwood and Glamorgan bowler John Mercer. Larwood, then 21 and weighing only 10 st. 8 lb. (67 kg) — he was 5 ft. 7½ in. (171cm) tall — was already showing the control and speed that eventually earned him 1427 wickets at an average of 17.51 in first-class cricket.

At the end of the tour it was announced that Sir Lindsay Parkinson had made Ponsford an offer to play with Blackpool, a Lancashire club, as an amateur. The idea of returning to England the following year appealed to Ponsford, but he didn't make an immediate decision as he wanted to discuss the matter with his wife Vera. After discussion the Ponsfords decided that Bill should remain in Melbourne in the winter of 1927.

The Australian team, which was not short of record-breakers, was able to sit back and enjoy a different kind of record before leaving England. From London's Paddington station, decorated with Australian flags in honour of the cricketers, the team travelled by train to Birkenhead. The train, bedecked in green and yellow, was drawn by an engine named the Windsor Castle and it covered the 210 miles (338 km) in three hours 55 minutes, reportedly a record for the journey. The first 123 miles (197 km) were covered in as many minutes. At Birkenhead the team left the train and crossed the Mersey River by ferry to Liverpool where it boarded the ship 'Montrose' for New York.

In New York the Australian players saw the New York Yankees and St Louis Cardinals playing in the 1926 World Series baseball. The Cardinals won the title 4–3 and, almost 60 years later, Ponsford vividly recalled Yankee star 'Babe' Ruth shaking his fist at an opposition pitcher for deliberately walking him. Another star to remain in Ponsford's memory was Yankee batter Lou Gehrig who established a record by playing 2130 consecutive games from 1925–39.

From New York, the Australian party travelled through Canada via the Rocky Mountains to Vancouver and then home by ship to finish a memorable tour.

NOTES

[1]Australia had won 13 Tests, lost one and drawn four, including eight wins in a row against England in seasons 1920–21 and 1921.

[2]Although short in stature, Charlie Macartney played the game with the presence of someone of high rank. This dominating attitude almost certainly led to the nickname 'The Governor-General'.

[3]Woodfull in 1930 equalled this feat of batting throughout the pre-lunch session on the first day of a Test while his partner hit a century. Again at Leeds he quietly played a minor role while Don Bradman reached 105 on his way to an epic 334.

[4]Late in the 1926 tour a second-class game was played against the Civil Service. By coincidence the captains were Herbie Collins and his brother, R.S. Collins.

HUNDREDS
AND THOUSANDS

I N the two seasons following the 1926 tour of England, Bill Ponsford enjoyed an astonishing run of success that made him the despair of bowlers and a batting phenomenon. Apart from breaking his own world record score, he hit more than 1000 runs in each season and at one stage had scored a century in 11 consecutive first-class games in Australia. Bill Woodfull did not score as heavily, but still produced more runs than most first-class players and with 'Ponny' formed a brilliant opening partnership.

On returning home from England, Woodfull was given a special welcome by the Carlton club on November 17. Among those present were Jack Ryder, former Test players John Blackham and Jack Worrall, and the Director of Education, Frank Tate. Mr Tate said the success gained by Woodfull in England had not gone to his head and he remained the man his contemporaries had always known. Woodfull returned to the teaching service, this time at Melbourne High School where he was to stay until the end of 1940.

Both Woodfull and Ponsford hit a century when they resumed with their clubs. Ponsford was in sparkling form against University, hitting 132 in 175 minutes with 10 fours and shots all around the wicket. Woodfull, who was given three cheers by the fielding side when he opened the innings at North Melbourne, began cautiously but then batted brightly for 103 in 162 minutes. His brother 'Jack', better known as a bowler, hit 60.

Neither Ponsford nor Woodfull had much time to settle in at home before they were again on the move, this time to Adelaide for Victoria's first Sheffield Shield match for 1926–27. It was a significant game for Woodfull, who had replaced the retired Mayne as captain. Victorian officials, impressed by Woodfull's success at home and abroad, not only appointed him captain but also asked him to share the duties of selection with Peter McAlister and Vernon Ransford. Obviously Woodfull, at 29, was a better choice in the long term than Jack Ryder, who was 37, although the latter had played more Tests and had captained Victoria when Mayne was absent.

Ryder made himself unavailable to play in Adelaide for business reasons and it was reported at the time that he would probably make few appearances for Victoria that season. Ryder was still an accomplished cricketer and, despite the choice of Woodfull as Victorian leader, he was destined to succeed Collins as Australia's captain in the 1928–29 series against England.

Woodfull had mixed fortunes on his first day as Victorian captain. He won the toss and batted in sultry conditions, opening with Ponsford, but with the total on 10 he was run out for one. Hendry made 30 and Mitchell 32, while 'Ponny' carried the innings. In one of his finest innings, possibly the best he ever played, Ponsford hit 214 of Victoria's 315 runs. First in and ninth out, caught by John Rymill off the bowling of Norman Williams, he was at the crease for only 267 minutes and hit 22 fours and a six. The innings was not the unique occasion that every batsman dreams of, but rather an indication of what was to come for the rest of the summer. Williams, an Adelaide dentist who always bowled wearing a cap, finished with six for 88.

South Australia replied with 481, both Rymill and Vic Richardson hitting centuries. Victoria began its second innings needing a good start from Ponsford and Woodfull to stay in the match. Ponsford contributed 54 and Woodfull made 84 before he was again run out, while Hendry hit a timely 177 to enable Victoria to reach 430. Williams added to his first innings success with six for 146. Vic Richardson also returned a fine double, his second innings score of 92 complementing his 137 earlier in the game.

Near the finish it seemed Victoria might score a thrilling win. When Cyril Parry[1] joined Grimmett at the fall of South Australia's eighth wicket, 18 runs were still needed for victory but the South Australian tailenders steered the score to eight for 267 to give their side a two-wicket win.

Victoria's batting power was evident against Shield newcomer Queensland at the MCG, leading the home State to victory by an innings and 169 runs. Rain washed out the first day of the game and then Queensland was all out for 147. Ponsford and Woodfull replied with an opening stand of 115 before Woodfull was bowled by Ron Oxenham for 56. Ponsford and Hendry then added 217 for the second wicket before 'Ponny' was out for 151. His bright innings had included 12 fours. Keith Rigg, a 20-year-old University batsman, following with 62 and Hendry reached 140 in the team's total of 533. Queensland made 217 in its second innings.

Greater opposition was expected from New South Wales in the match at the MCG starting on Christmas Eve, a Friday, although for one reason or another, New South Wales was drained of much of its former strength. There was no Collins, Macartney or Kelleway, nor did Jack Gregory, Oldfield or Everett play. But New South Wales had a fine captain in Kippax and experienced men such as Mailey and Andrews played.

On the first day, before a crowd of 8174, New South Wales made only 221 in a disappointing effort. There was no play at the weekend and when the game resumed on Monday December 27 a crowd of 22,893 saw an incredible day of cricket. Woodfull, who opened with Ponsford, was the only batsman dismissed. He was out for a solid 133, caught at the wicket off Andrews, when the total was 375. This remained the highest opening stand in a Sheffield Shield match until 1982–83 when Robbie Kerr and Kepler Wessels hit 388 for Queensland against Victoria. Ponsford, who had passed 200, continued to make merry and became the first and only player to hit 300 in a day at the MCG. By stumps he was 334 with Hendry a useful 86 not out and the Victorian total a staggering one for 573.[2]

The next day a slightly larger crowd totalling 23,348 turned up in anticipation of more records. Clem Hill's Shield record of 365 not out wasn't far off and the possibility of Ponsford making another 400 was distinct. Hendry had reached 100 when he became the second batsman dismissed, having helped 'Ponny' add 219 for the second wicket in less than two hours. Ponsford, who was joined by Ryder, was picking up runs carefully but with his own score on 352 and the total 614 'Ponny' played on to Morgan and his grand innings was finished. He had gathered his runs in only 363 minutes and struck 36 fours. It was estimated that he had run eight kilometres while at the crease, partly because Woodfull had hit only seven boundaries and Hendry five.

Love and King were both out cheaply, stumped off Mailey, but the run spree continued when Ryder was joined by Hartkopf. The pair added 177 for the sixth wicket, Hartkopf's share being 61. Ryder had reached 100 in 115 minutes and was on his way to a second hundred, completed in 74 minutes. His batting was even quicker and more exciting than Ponsford's, especially when he decided to hit the ball over the boundary rather than along the ground.

Many years later Woodfull described Ryder's innings as 'the most terrific hitting seen in cricket' and added that when Kippax had been assured by leg-spinner Andrews that he knew enough about Ryder to dismiss him in an over, Ryder increased his scoring rate at Andrews' expense. He was also severe on Mailey, hitting a towering six which struck the verandah on the smokers' pavilion.[3] In all he hit six sixes, but it was Andrews who had the last laugh.

At 275 Ryder faced Andrews and hit the first delivery for four. The next went for six, followed by another four and a six. The fifth ball he mis-hit and Kippax took the catch. Ryder's 295 had taken only 245 minutes and he had sped from 200 in 56 minutes. Meanwhile, Jack Ellis had hit Victoria's one thousandth run and he and Blackie added 71 for the last wicket. The total of 1107 broke Victoria's world record score of 1059 which was amassed on the same ground several years earlier against Tasmania.

The historic Victorian innings was:

W. WOODFULL, c Ratcliffe, b Andrews	133
W. PONSFORD, b Morgan	352
H. HENDRY, c Morgan, b Mailey	100
J. RYDER, c Kippax, b Andrews	295
H. LOVE, stpd. Ratcliffe, b Mailey	6
S. KING, stpd. Ratcliffe, b Mailey	7
A. HARTKOPF, c McGuirk, b Mailey	61
A. LIDDICUT, b McGuirk	36
J. ELLIS, run out	63
F. MORTON, run out	0
D. BLACKIE, not out	27
Sundries	27
Total	1107

Fall: 375, 594, 614, 631, 657, 834, 915, 1043, 1046, 1107.

BOWLING

	Overs	Maidens	Runs	Wickets
McNamee	24	2	124	0
McGuirk	26	1	130	1
Mailey	64	0	362	4
Campbell	11	0	89	0
Phillips	11.7	0	64	0
Morgan	26	0	137	1
Andrews	21	2	148	2
Kippax	7	0	26	0

On the fourth day approximately 6000 people attended the MCG to watch New South Wales bat a second time. Hartkopf took six for 98 and the innings was wound up for 230, leaving Victoria the winner by an innings and 656 runs.

The crowds were back at the MCG on New Year's Day 1927 when the match against South Australia began. Victoria batted first and although Woodfull was out for six, Ponsford hit 108 and Hendry 68 in a total of 304. Frank Morton, who had come to Victoria from South Australia that season, captured five for 70 against his former State which managed only 148 in all.

Ponsford and Woodfull began Victoria's second innings with a stand of 104, of which the latter made 34. Ponsford was out for 84, lbw to Grimmett. On the second day 30,219 people saw the game and a further 12,036 came on the third day when Love and Hartkopf each made a century. Rain spoiled the fourth day and Victoria's massive second innings of 649 left South Australia 805 to win. Naturally that was never possible and the visitors were all out for 233, Morton again taking bowling honours with four for 70.

The importance of Ponsford and Woodfull to the Victorian team was particularly evident when one or the other was unavailable. Neither played in the next match, against New South Wales in Sydney, for different reasons. A change of personnel at the head office of the State Savings Bank had made it hard for Ponsford to obtain leave to play cricket[4] and Woodfull was being married.

In addition to the two opening batsmen, Ryder declared himself unavailable and Hartkopf and Love also stayed behind. There were reports at the time that members of the 1926 team which toured England were not happy with the Board of Control's bonus of £250 ($500 — a useful handout at the time) and would not play further Shield games unless given £300 ($600).

On January 12 1927 Bill Woodfull began another long and worthy partnership when he married Gwen King. The pair had met about five years earlier when Gwen had been a member of the choir at Rev Woodfull's Albert Park church. Born at Albert Park, Miss King lived in Beaconsfield Parade on the foreshore of Hobson's Bay. Her father, John King, was a grocer's sundries manufacturer and flour miller with an office in Bay Street Port Melbourne, where she worked as his secretary. Gwen's brother, John, played cricket with a church team, but the Kings were not steeped in cricket.

Gwen King soon learned the finer points of the game as she watched her future husband playing club matches with South Melbourne and later Carlton, as well as his appearances with Victoria at the

MCG. By the time she married, Gwen had a considerable under-standing of the game. Fresh in her memory was the partnership of 375 between her fiance and Ponsford which she had watched at the MCG.

Hunter Hendry captained Victoria in the absence of Woodfull and seldom have fortunes in sport been reversed in such a short time. New South Wales, mercilessly beaten a month earlier, humiliated Victoria. Batting first, the home State compiled a strong 469, due largely to Kippax's 217 not out. Victoria was two for 16 when rain stopped play on the second day.

Bearing in mind that Victoria had made 1107 in its previous innings, it was bewildering to see it collapse to seven for 19 on (black) Friday January 28, 1927. Caught on a rain-affected pitch, the Victorians couldn't handle paceman Ray McNamee who took seven for 21 and veteran slow bowler Charles Macartney who grabbed three for 10. It was left to number 11 batsman Bert Davie, a former Tasmanian playing with Prahran, to top score with 10 not out in a grand total of 35.

Kippax must have had great delight in asking Hendry, a former New South Wales representative, to follow on. Davie was promoted from rabbit to opener and justified the move by making 15 before edging Macartney to Oldfield. Arthur Liddicut scored a valiant 55, but Victoria again folded to be all out for 181. Mullett, the left-arm medium-pace bowler from Essendon, made a king pair. Early in the game he had taken two wickets, including that of Johnny Taylor.

Beaten by an innings and 253 runs, Victoria was in trouble as it now needed to beat Queensland in Brisbane to win the Shield. Ponsford helped by gaining leave from his bank, but another disaster followed after Queensland had scored a first innings 399. The pitch was sound, but the batting wasn't and Victoria collapsed to be all out for 86. Ponsford made 12.

Queensland did not enforce the follow-on and made 439, giving Victoria the hopeless task of making 753 to win the game and the Shield. Ponsford and Hendry decided it was worth a try and set about the job with a century stand. They were still together at 200 and weren't parted until the score reached 225. Ponsford (116) and Hendry (137) were supported by Fred Baring, who hit 73, and Keith Millar (64). This lifted Victoria's second innings total to a very respec-table 518, but Queensland won the match by 234 runs, giving South Australia the Shield. It was the first time Queensland had beaten Victoria in Brisbane and only its second win since the pair first met in 1903.

Ponsford and Woodfull played one more first-class game for the season and both were in grand form. Playing for an Australian XI against The Rest in Sydney — a testimonial for Charles Macartney — they put on 223 for the first wicket, Woodfull making 140 and Ponsford 131. It was Ponsford's sixth century in six first-class games that season. Tommy Andrews, who made an unfinished 115, was the third century-maker in a total of 533. Williams was the best bowler with six for 174.

In the second innings Ponsford needed 25 to beat Victor Trumper's record of 1246 runs for an Australian season, set in 1910–11, but he was out for seven. Trumper had batted 20 times at an average of 69.22, whereas Ponsford's 1229 runs had been made in 10 innings at an average of 122.90.

Resuming club games with St Kilda, Ponsford continued his phenomenal form and it was no surprise that he headed the VCA averages with 779 runs at 111.28 per innings. Woodfull was third with 457 runs at 91.4. Ponsford's first game with St Kilda after the first-class season was at North Melbourne, where he hit a chanceless 202 not out in 188 minutes, including 24 fours. Ponsford, who shared an opening stand of 155 with Bert Cohen (55), sped to his first hundred in 109 minutes and his second in only 72 minutes.

Meanwhile, Woodfull had to wait until the following Saturday for a bat against Hawthorn-East Melbourne. Shedding his usual caution he raced to 142 in only 137 minutes. Against Melbourne he was in similar form, hitting an unconquered 125 in 139 minutes in the second innings after a duck in the first. Ponsford looked set for another big innings when he had scored 27 in 29 minutes against South Melbourne, but was out to a fine catch when trying to cover drive. That completed the home and away games and the same teams met in a semi-final. By a strange coincidence the other semi-finalists, Collingwood and Hawthorn-East Melbourne, had also met in the last home and away game.

Ponsford was again in magnificent form and combined with Fred Yeomans to add 472 for the second wicket. The game started with the customary good opening from Ponsford and Cohen, the partnership being broken at 60 when the latter batsman was out for 24. Yeomans joined Ponsford and, despite an easy chance given by 'Ponny' when 103, the partnership remained intact at stumps with St Kilda one for 355. Ponsford was 200 and Yeomans 112.

At the resumption of play on Easter Monday, the pair took the score to 532 before Yeomans was bowled by Frank Morton for 186. Soon after, Ponsford was caught by Roy Park on the leg side for

295. He had batted for 362 minutes and hit 33 fours and one six. St Kilda declared at stumps on the second day, having scored eight for 664. In reply, Lawson (121) and Park (78) gave South Melbourne a start of 207 but the succeeding batsmen fell cheaply and the innings ended at 297 on the fourth day.

St Kilda met Collingwood in the final at St Kilda and it was no surprise that the Saints won their fourth consecutive flag. Nor was it a surprise that their first innings total reached 557. The one surprise was that Ponsford was out for eight but Guthrie (178), Eaton (160) and Yeomans (84) showed that the team did not rely on one player. Ponsford made 39 and Cohen top-scored with 114 in St Kilda's second innings of 256. Collingwood made 233 and none for 22.

The Mayor of St Kilda, Cr Dawkins, unfurled the flag the following October before the start of St Kilda's opening game for 1927–28, against Prahran. The St Kilda City brass band supported the occasion as did Bill Ponsford who reeled off 188 in 217 minutes despite a slow outfield. His innings included 12 fours and eight threes.

Woodfull also began the new season with a century, hitting a chanceless 128 not out in 225 minutes against Collingwood. Both he and Ponsford were among the runs when Carlton played St Kilda the next month. The pitch was slow and the outfield heavy, but Ponsford made light of the conditions with an unbeaten 165 in St Kilda's innings of four for 301, which was closed early on the second day. Carlton replied with an opening stand worth 142 between Bill Woodfull and H. De Gruchy. Woodfull took only two hours to make 84 and his partner contributed 56, but the game was drawn with Carlton scoring six for 204.

St Kilda then had a bye and used the free time to visit Hobart for a game against southern Tasmania. Ponsford was the star, making 105 before he was run out. Woodfull missed his scheduled match with Carlton owing to a family bereavement and it was then time to begin the quest for the Sheffield Shield, against South Australia in Adelaide.

The Ponsford-Woodfull combination, which in 1926–27 had become a formidable partnership, was again strong and wasn't separated until the second ball after lunch when Woodfull was caught off Grimmett for 43 with the total at 97. The Victorian captain had batted for 98 minutes without hitting a boundary. Ponsford batted a further 110 minutes and did not give a chance in compiling 133.

Hendry, missed in the slips before scoring, hit 168 and Hartkopf also made a century in Victoria's innings total of eight for 646 (dec.). In reply, South Australia was bundled out for 177 and 159 to leave

Victoria the winner by an innings and 310 runs.

Ponsford's penchant for a huge score was again evident in the next match when Queensland captain and wicketkeeper Leo O'Connor surprisingly asked Victoria to bat on a hot day after he had won the toss. Ponsford and Woodfull had pushed the score to 74 when the latter drove hard into the covers but was run out for 31. Hendry joined Ponsford and the pair steadily built a massive total. After 267 minutes Ponsford reached 200. Hendry completed his eighth century in only three years with his adopted State, and when he was bowled by Gough for 129 he had helped Ponsford add 314 for the second wicket.

At stumps Victoria was two for 400, with Ponsford on 234 and Ryder four. On resumption, a large crowd watched Ryder advance to 70 and Ponsford, with superb placement of the ball, completed his second quadruple century. With Ryder out, wickets were falling more frequently and there were doubts that Ponsford would have the partners to give him the chance to break his score of 429 made against Tasmania. Fortunately the innings continued long enough for him to beat his own world record. At 437 he hit a return catch to Queensland bowler G. S. Amos and soon after Victoria was all out for 793. Ponsford had made his runs in 621 minutes, clubbing 42 fours in the process. Perhaps Archie MacLaren at last recognised that there was a better batsman than himself. By coincidence Ponsford scored 42 boundaries in both world record efforts.

Ponsford had also broken Hill's Shield record of 365 not out and it now only remained for him to beat R. E. Foster's Test record of 287 for England versus Australia in 1903–04. Curiously, while Ponsford was covering himself with glory in Melbourne, a 19-year-old New South Welshman playing his first first-class game was on his way to a chanceless 118 in Adelaide. His name was Don Bradman and he, rather than Ponsford, was destined to surpass Foster's Test record.[5]

Victoria, having disposed of Queensland for 189 and 407, now faced New South Wales at the MCG. The brilliant Victorian openers were still together at lunch with 117 to their credit, of which Ponsford had made 62 and Woodfull 54. After the break Ponsford shot ahead of his partner and completed yet another century. Woodfull, too, was on the verge of a three-figure score when he played a poor stroke back to McNamee who caught him for 99. Woodfull had batted for three hours and shared a first-wicket stand of 227.

McNamee gained another prize when he had Hendry caught at the wicket for nought in the same over. The irrepressible Ponsford continued to pour forth runs in a great quantity, but with the total at five for 340 his grand innings ended at 202 when he was caught by Bradman. It was Bradman's first catch in first-class cricket. Ponsford had batted for 286 minutes and hit 18 boundaries. Once he was out, McNamee wrapped up the Victorian innings for 355 at a personal cost of seven for 77.

New South Wales led by 12 runs after Andrews (110) and Morgan (93) had batted well. Bradman made a useful 31. With the game evenly balanced, Ponsford and Woodfull gave their side a start of 71 in the second innings before 'Ponny' was bowled by McNamee for 38. Woodfull accumulated runs at a steady pace and was unbeaten on 191 when he declared at seven for 386. He had batted 281 minutes and had reached the boundary only 10 times.

The problem of batting last manifested itself when New South Wales crumbled for 152, failing to handle Blackie who returned the outstanding figures of six for 32. Andrews again top-scored, this time with 53.

Having beaten New South Wales by a clear-cut margin of 222 runs, Victoria confidently went into the New Year's game against South Australia at the MCG. Ponsford and Woodfull sent their side off to another great start, scoring 236 by the time 'Woody' was out for 106. Ponsford, the MCG's resident run machine, completed his fourth triple century on the Melbourne ground with an innings of 336. His feat beat the previous world record of three triple centuries by W. G. Grace. In four hands at the MCG that season he had hit a remarkable 1013 runs and his latest century was his eleventh in 11 games in Australia since February 1926. Having not long turned 27 he had many years of cricket ahead of him.

Ponsford's 336, which was also the highest individual score in games between Victoria and South Australia, enabled Victoria to reach 637 to which South Australia answered with 319 and 283. At that stage Ponsford and Woodfull had scored 1616 of Victoria's 2817 runs for the season.

How much longer could the amazing sequence of big scores go on? Ponsford was entitled to the occasional off day, but the New South Wales Cricket Association believed in being positive and had posters printed advising the public that the world's greatest batsman would be at the cricket ground when New South Wales met Victoria. The posters were pinned to telegraph poles in the city and suburbs to advertise the fact.

Those who attended the Sydney Cricket Ground (SCG) in anticipation of more Ponsford records were disappointed, but the brief lapse by the great batsman could hardly be held against him. In both the first and second innings he had to bow to the brilliance of that splendid all-rounder Jack Gregory, who bowled him for six in the first instance and then caught him, where others could well have missed, for two in the second innings. It was a case of one champion showing his worth at the expense of another.

Woodfull, on the other hand, had a productive match with scores of 94 and 81 not out in a drawn game. In the first innings he shared a stand of 192 with Hendry, who was also on 94 when Woodfull was out. Hendry went on to make 138 against his former team[6].

Woodfull was forced to withdraw from the match against Queensland in Brisbane because of an injured knee. In a rain-interrupted game, which did not prevent Victoria winning the Sheffield Shield, Ponsford hit 63 in his side's first innings total of 300. Queensland was nine for 384 when the game finished.

Ponsford had hit 1217 runs in eight innings, a Shield record that stood until 1982–83 when Victorian batsman Graham Yallop hit 1254. Significantly, Yallop batted 18 times.

After their highly successful season with Victoria, Ponsford and Woodfull toured New Zealand with an Australian team lead by Vic Richardson. Woodfull was vice-captain and other members of the party were Archie Jackson, Kippax, Oldfield, Grimmett, Blackie, McNamee, Oxenham, Schneider, Morton and Colin Alexander.

Both Ponsford and Woodfull played six first-class games, including two unofficial Tests, with Woodfull the more successful of the pair. His 781 runs, at an average of 130.16, included a career highest of 284 in the first unofficial Test. After his fantastic success in Australia over the previous two seasons, Ponsford made a handy 452 runs which yielded an average of 56.50. By comparison with his earlier efforts he had dropped back to the ruck, but it would be unfair to have expected him to continue to hit a century in every game. Ponsford simply became a good batsman again after a spell as a superhuman player.

Twice in matches against the provinces, Ponsford and Woodfull sent the tourists away to a three-figure start. Against Wellington they shared a stand worth 122 in only 95 minutes, Ponsford being bowled for 58 and Woodfull building his score to 165 before he was caught. At Dunedin the pair had scored 214 against Otago when Woodfull was out for 107. Ponsford had his best innings of the tour, reaching 148, and like Woodfull was caught Alloo, bowled Dickinson. Otago replied to the Australian score of 454 with 171 and when the tourists batted a second time they were on 75 runs with all wickets intact when rain washed out play. Ponsford was on 54 and Schneider 17.

The first 'Test' was drawn. It began in Auckland within a week of aviator Bert Hinkler's landing at Flemington racecourse after his history-making flight from England. Australia was a commanding two for 416 at stumps on the first day after Ponsford and Woodfull had shared an opening partnership of 184. 'Ponny' was the first out, caught for 86, but Woodfull was still there at the end of the day with 250 beside his name. The following day he was bowled for 284 in a total of five for 573 (dec.). New Zealand replied with 288 and one for 53. The match was drawn.

The Australians won the second 'Test', in Dunedin, by seven wickets. New Zealand was all out for 162, due mainly to Grimmett taking six for 47 against the land of his birth. By stumps on the opening day the tourists were in trouble at four for 57, Ponsford (13) and Woodfull (15) both being bowled cheaply. An unbeaten 46 from Ron Oxenham enabled the innings to reach 188, but the locals managed only 154 in their second knock. Blackie (five for 27) and Grimmett (three for 63) did the damage. The Australians scored the necessary 129 for victory with the loss of three wickets. Ponsford was bowled for 30 and Woodfull made 45 not out.

The tour of New Zealand did not cost either Ponsford or Woodfull the chance of playing in the VCA finals, as neither player's club reached the final four. Woodfull headed the VCA averages with an imposing 133.00 from three innings. Ponsford batted five times for an average of 121.00.

NOTES

[1]Parry, South Australia's wicketkeeper, later lived in Melbourne and was coach of Northcote Cricket Club in the 1950s. He died in 1984, aged 83.

[2]Only Charles Macartney, who scored 345 for the Australians against Nottinghamshire in 1921, has scored more runs in a day than Ponsford in a first-class game.

[3]On the site of today's Members' stand.

[4]Later in 1927 Ponsford took up a five-year contract with the *Herald* newspaper, as a public relations officer.

[5]Andy Sandham broke the record in 1929–30 with 325 for England against the West Indies, but held it for only a few months before Bradman hit 334 for Australia against England at Leeds.

[6]Hendry was one of eight century-makers in that game. The others were Ryder (106), Rigg (110n.o.) for Victoria, and Kippax (134), Bradman (134n.o.), Morgan (110), Nicholls (119) and Oldfield (101) for New South Wales.

BROKEN BONES

A sportsman is lucky if he endures a career of a decade or longer without a serious injury. In successive years, both Ponsford and Woodfull broke bones in their hands, causing each to miss much of the season. Ponsford was hurt during a Test series against England and Woodfull's injury occurred within five months of the 1930 tour of England. Ponsford had batted eight times in 1928–29 before being injured and already had an unbeaten 275 to his credit. By coincidence Woodfull's highest score that season was also 275 not out.

Opening day of the 1928–29 season was a particularly happy one for St Kilda's new captain, Bill Ponsford. His son Bill was born that morning, the first of Bill and Vera Ponsford's two sons, and to celebrate, the proud father hit 77 against South Melbourne. Meanwhile, Bill Woodfull began the new season in equally good form, hitting 120 in 190 minutes against Fitzroy, his cutting and straight driving highlighting the innings.

There was little time for club cricket before a Test trial was played at the MCG between an Australian XI and The Rest. Ponsford and Woodfull scored 100 of the Australian XI's 398 (79 and 21 respectively) and did not get a second hit as The Rest made only 111 and 244 against the bowling of Ron Oxenham and Grimmett. (Their match figures were 10 for 90 and seven for 154 respectively.) Don Bradman made 14 and five for The Rest.

The match did little to enhance Australia's chances against the visiting England team which was one of the strongest to tour Australia, under the captaincy of Percy Chapman. Woodfull stepped aside as

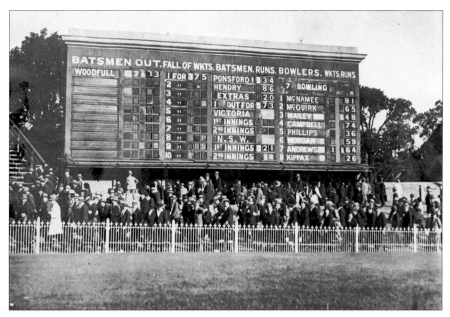

The Melbourne Cricket Ground scoreboard at the end of the second day's play in the Christmas, 1926 game between Victoria and New South Wales. Victoria, which had begun its first innings at the start of the day, was 1/573. Ponsford who had scored 334, went on to make 352 and Victoria reached 1107.

The Australians during their 1928 tour of New Zealand. Back row (left to right) Karl Schneider, Ron Oxenham, W.C. Alexander, W.C. Bull (manager), Frank Morton, Don Blackie, Archie Jackson.
Front row (left to right) Ray McNamee, Clarrie Grimmett, Bert Oldfield, Vic Richardson (captain), Bill Woodfull (vice captain), Alan Kippax, Bill Ponsford.

Bill and Gwen Woodfull on their wedding day.

The picturesque Worcester ground where Woodfull hit a century at the start of the 1930 tour.

Victorian captain to allow Jack Ryder, the new Australian Test captain in place of the retired Collins, to lead his State.

Victoria's first meeting with the MCC in Melbourne was notable for a number of reasons. Harold Larwood made his first appearance at the MCG and took seven for 51; colourful cockney batsman 'Patsy' Hendren hit his hundredth first-class century when he made an even 100; Woodfull carried his bat and Douglas Jardine, also making his debut at the MCG, hit 104.

Batting first, Victoria was all out for 164 in 194 minutes. Woodfull was the only player who did not succumb to paceman Larwood and remained 67 not out at the end of the innings. Ponsford, playing his hundredth first-class innings, was bowled by Larwood for 14. England replied with a commanding 486, Larwood was run out for a most useful 79.

Woodfull, suffering with influenza, was unable to bat in Victoria's second innings, so Hendry opened with Ponsford in his stead. Hendry survived a snick to slips off the first ball from Tate and by stumps on the third day he was 74 and 'Ponny' 60 in a Victorian score of 135. There was no further play due to rain.

After falling for seven in Victoria's first innings against South Australia at the MCG, Ponsford was back to his familiar brilliance in the second innings. Batting for only five and a half hours he remained unconquered on 275 when the innings was closed at four for 464. Ponsford hit 30 fours and one six and shared a third-wicket partnership of 249 with Keith Rigg who hit 90.

Woodfull did not play following his attack of influenza, but a week later made 68 for Carlton against St Kilda.

The first Test, also the first played in Brisbane, was a debacle as far as Australia was concerned. England won by a massive 675 runs and, sadly, Jack Gregory did not play again after hurting a knee. While it was Gregory's last Test, it was Bradman's first.

England proved its batting depth when it batted first, hitting 521 of which Hendren contributed 169. Australia replied with a miserable 122. Woodfull failed to score and Ponsford made two. Both wickets fell to Larwood. Bradman, batting at number 7 in his first Test, hit 18. Chapman did not enforce the follow-on and declared England's second innings at eight for 342, leaving australia 742 to win.

It was a next-to-impossible task, made all the more hopeless because Gregory and Kelleway were indisposed and could not bat. Nevertheless, Australia should have done better than the disaster that followed. Only Woodfull emerged with his head unbowed. His application to the circumstances proved that a side did not have to capitulate because the opposition had it on the run. Admittedly there had been rain overnight, but it was thought that if the early batsmen could hold out, the bowlers would not be dangerous.

'Old Boy' of the *Argus* described the pitch as 'not good, but it could not be called really bad'. He went on to say, 'Woodfull was an object lesson to all the others. He stood up to his work like a Trojan. He was always over and behind the ball, and he stuck to the very end, thus repeating his performance in Melbourne (of carrying his bat).

'We have pampered our batsmen for so many years that when they do strike a wicket that is not plumb, they are all at sea. We seldom see batsmen practising on a wicket that is worn or rain-damaged, with the result that when they do have to play on one in a match they are powerless.'

Australia, one for 17 overnight, having lost Ponsford for six, resumed with Woodfull and Kippax. They took the score to 33 before the New South Welshman played a poor shot and skied the ball back to Larwood. Hendry, after making six, skied a ball off White and Australia was three for 46. Ryder had made only one when he stepped out to drive Tate, but he mis-hit the ball to Larwood at mid-on and another wicket was down. Bradman played a bad stroke to be caught at point and the score had sagged to five for 49, effectively seven for 49 with Gregory and Kelleway absent.

Woodfull, unperturbed, batted on with great resolution. Oldfield joined him, but managed only five runs before he was back in the pavilion with the total at 62. Woodfull continued to present the full face of the bat to the ball and held firm. To his credit, Grimmett tried to emulate his partner's attitude but he wasn't up to the task and left when the score reached 66. Ironmonger followed on the next ball.

Woodfull, who remained 30 not out, had carried his bat, but England had won the Test by a staggering 675 runs. England's captain, Percy Chapman, believed that the covering of pitches for Sheffield Shield games had deprived the Australian batsmen of the experience they needed to cope with an uncovered pitch. He pointed out that Woodfull had shown that the pitch was playable. Ryder told reporters that the pitch was a credit to the curator, thus laying the blame for Australia's downfall squarely on the shoulders of the Australian batsmen.

The second Test, in Sydney, began on Friday December 13 in front of a crowd of 40,723. Bradman was dropped to twelfth man and Australia opened with Woodfull and Vic Richardson. Ponsford came in at number four. Following the debacle in Brisbane, it was refreshing to find the openers had completed a half-century partnership before Richardson was bowled by Larwood for 27. Kippax did not last long and Ponsford had made five when he was hit on a hand by a delivery from Larwood which badly broke a bone. He was forced to retire. The injury precluded Ponsford from the rest of the series, which greatly affected Australia's chances of recovery from its disastrous start.

With the total on 152, Woodfull was lbw to Geary for a valuable 68. He had batted for 173 minutes and was to remain the only player to pass 40 as the innings folded for 253. The next day a capacity crowd of 58,446 jammed the SCG and the visiting batsmen began an innings which yielded 636. Walter Hammond, a stroke-maker of the highest class and destined to become one of England's greatest players, was the hero with 251. Hendren (74) and Geary (66) also did well.

Australia's woes continued when Richardson was out for no score in the second innings, but a second-wicket stand of 215 between Woodfull and Hendry added much life to a game in danger of becoming as one-sided as the first Test. The partnership was broken when Hendry was lbw to Tate for 112. Woodfull was on 111 when he patted the ball in front of the wicket and started to run. Kippax, the non-striker, did not move and Woodfull was unable to regain his crease before Tate smartly fielded and Duckworth broke the wicket. Woodfull had batted for 258 minutes and hit six fours. By this time the total stood at 234.

A valuable 79 from Ryder and a useful 44 from Queenslander Otto Nothling enabled Australia, batting a man short, to avoid an innings defeat and post a sound total of 397. England scored two for 16 in its second innings to win by eight wickets.

At this stage Australia, without Ponsford, needed to win all three remaining Tests to win the Ashes. While it didn't achieve this remote goal, Australia did at least show considerable improvement as the series advanced and won the fifth Test by five wickets after narrowly losing the fourth.

Australia was off to a shaky start in the third Test, in Melbourne, losing Woodfull for seven and Richardson for three with only 15 runs scored. Kippax and Ryder led a fine recovery, each scoring a century, and Bradman gave strong support with 79. A world record crowd of 63,247 watched the first day's play and 62,259 watched the second day's play. Chasing Australia's total of 397, England led by 20 thanks to a double century from Hammond. Don Blackie, the

46-year-old St Kilda off-spinner, who had a long career with Prahran, was Australia's best bowler (six for 94).

Richardson was again out cheaply in Australia's second innings, but Woodfull and Hendry became associated with what promised to be another big partnership. Woodfull, outscoring his partner by three runs to one, played a very fine hand. Hendry was out, stumped Duckworth off 'Farmer' White for 12 when the total was 60. Soon after Woodfull reached 50 in only 81 minutes and, with Kippax, added a further 58 runs by stumps. The next day the pair added a further 20 before the New South Welshman was bowled by Tate for 41. Ryder made only five runs before playing on to the bowling of Geary.

At four for 143 Bradman joined Woodfull and marked his return to the Test team with some resolute batting. The loss of Kippax and Ryder caused Woodfull and Bradman to exercise great care and the scoring rate dropped. After 259 minutes at the crease Woodfull reached his century and a moment later called for a new bat. He was out soon after for 107 when he played forward to a good-length ball from Tate and edged it to Duckworth.

Bradman went on to complete his maiden Test century (112) and enabled Australia to reach a sound total of 351. England, needing 332 to win, was no certainty although a start of 105 from Hobbs and Sutcliffe took much pressure off the later batsmen. Sutcliffe top-scored with 135 and England won by three wickets, a comfortable but by no means conclusive win when compared with the previous two results.

The fourth Test in Adelaide, like its counterpart four years earlier, was one of the greatest Tests played. England eventually won by 12 runs, but it is interesting to speculate over what might have happened had Bradman escaped being run out in Australia's second innings. The most pleasing aspect for Australia was that it was now back on level terms with its old rival.

England batted first and despite a 143-run start from Hobbs and Sutcliffe, and an unbeaten 119 by Hammond, was held to a total of 334. Grimmett finished with five for 102 for Australia. By contrast Australia began poorly, losing Woodfull for one, Hendry for two and Kippax for three with only 19 scored, yet recovered to compile 369 and lead by 35 on the first innings. This was due to the wonderful effort of 19-year-old Scots-born Archie Jackson who gave a chanceless display in making 164[1].

Jackson and Ryder, who made 63, added 126 for the fourth wicket and Bradman followed with a handy 40. When England batted a second time, Hammond continued his superb form making his second century of the match and his fourth for the series. Hammond's 177 was the basis of his team's total of 383, which left Australia 349 to win.

The target was not beyond Australia's batting capabilities although in the fourth innings of the game the odds favoured England. Following his brilliant display in the first innings, Jackson again opened with Woodfull and the pair put on 65 before Jackson was out for 36. Hendry joined Woodfull but only six more had been added when the latter was out for 30, a patient innings lasting 116 minutes. The loss of Hendry for five meant that Kippax and Ryder needed to stay together for some time to give Australia a chance of winning. Ryder made 87 and Kippax 51, in a partnership of 137. By the end of the sixth day Australia, at six for 260, had an excellent chance of winning the game, while Bradman was still at the crease.

Bradman and Oxenham took the score past 300, which meant that Australia needed less than 50 to win with four wickets standing. At 308 Oxenham was out for 12 and Oldfield joined Bradman. The pair pushed the scored along to 320 and the chances of an England win receded each time the young New South Welshman pierced the field. Then came the turning point in the game. Bradman attempted an impossible single and was run out for 58.

Australia needed 29 runs to win and England needed two wickets. Grimmett joined Oldfield and they pared 16 off the deficit before the former was caught off the bowling of White. Blackie came in, but was dismissed by White without scoring. White finished with eight for 126 from 64.5 overs and England had won by a slender 12 runs.

Two points of interest arose after the fourth Test. Firstly, Hammond had an amazing average of 141.8 in the four Tests to date and the game's authorities felt that too long was being taken to complete the Tests. They decided to limit each Test to six days between the hours of 12 noon and 6 p.m.

As a prelude to the fifth and final Test, Victoria met the MCC for a second time. The match was merely a formality as the Ashes had been won and the Englishmen hardly needed match practice or the chance to experiment. With so little at stake it was unfortunate that an incident took place involving Larwood and the Melbourne crowd.

Woodfull was on the verge of carrying his bat for the third time that season against the tourists, being 275 not out when Ironmonger came in at number 11. The end was indeed in sight as Ironmonger was not renowned for staying around, yet Chapman called on Larwood to bowl. The crowd greeted the move with derision. Here was the world's best fast bowler being used to remove the batsman least likely to score a run for Victoria.

Larwood took it seriously and bowled off a long run to a strong off-side field. 'Dainty' Ironmonger also took it seriously and clipped the first delivery for two. He scored another two off the next ball and survived a scorching third delivery outside the off stump. By now the crowd was ecstatic; it roared as Larwood ran in for his fourth ball. Larwood, obviously affected by the crowd's mood, stopped and then walked over to Chapman, throwing the ball to him.

Chapman gave it back, urging him to get on with the game. Larwood obeyed but as he ran in to bowl, the crowd sensed he was rattled and began baiting him. Again he stopped at the crease and the fieldsmen sat down. By his actions, Larwood was saying to the crowd 'if you shut up we'll play ball'. But the crowd kept on heckling and three times Larwood ran in, then stopped. Each time the players sat down.

Woodfull spoke to Chapman and together they walked to the noisy crowd in front of the Wardill stand[2] to reason with the barrackers. Their efforts were wasted, but Ryder defused the situation by declaring the innings closed at nine for 572. Chapman had been within his rights in bowling Larwood. After all, the innings had lasted 460 minutes and it wasn't a bad idea to wind it up as quickly as possible. As a professional cricketer Larwood was childish in letting the crowd get the better of him. Sooner or later he would have removed Ironmonger and it's to his discredit that he didn't accept the batsman's rare moment of success and get on with the job. To Ryder's credit he saved any further trouble, but poor Woodfull missed out on carrying his bat.

England replied with 303 and three for 308 and the match was drawn.

Centuries to Hobbs (142) and Maurice Leyland (137) opened the fifth Test at the MCG and England's first innings total of 519 seemed an insurance against defeat. Australia began its long chase with a handy start of 54 between Woodfull and Jackson before the latter was run out for 30. Woodfull had correctly called Jackson for a run after Jackson had played a stroke through the gully. Unfortunately the batsman stumbled as he started off on the run and Larwood's return beat him home.

Woodfull continued to bat well and with Kippax (38) added 89 for the second wicket. At stumps on the third day the Victorian was 78 not out, an invaluable knock under the circumstances. The next day he completed his third century of the series and was out soon after for 102, patiently made in five and a half hours. Bradman and New South Wales all-rounder Alan Fairfax added 183 for the fifth wicket, scoring 123 and 65, respectively. Australia's batting, especially that of Woodfull and Bradman, enabled the team to reach 491.

England, leading by only 28, did not fare particularly well in its second innings and late on the sixth day was all out for 257. This left Australia 286 to win, a formidable but by no means impossible task. Oldfield and Percy Hornibrook were sent in as nightwatchmen and at stumps Australia was none for seven. The pair provided a bonus the next day as the first wicket didn't fall until the score was on 51, when Hornibrook was bowled by Hammond for 18. Hammond also bowled Oldfield, for 48, with the total on 80 and, at 129 he bowled Woodfull for 35. Woodfull, who had been very solid, was a big loss for Australia and there was now a chance that England could even make a clean sweep of the series as Australia had done in 1920–21.

Jackson contributed a handy 46 and at stumps the home team was four for 173 with Kippax and Ryder at the crease and the brilliant young Bradman still to come. Australia resumed batting on the eighth day with six wickets in hand and 113 runs needed to win. There was a setback at 201 when Kippax was run out for 28, but Bradman joined his skipper and between them they hit off the required runs to give Australia a five-wicket win. Ryder was 57 not out and Bradman 37 not out at the finish.

There were no Test matches in the 1929–30 season although a visiting MCC team led by Harold Gilligan, brother of former England captain Arthur Gilligan, played matches against the States. The season began with a number of changes at club level. A new team, VCA Colts, was admitted to give the District competition 14 clubs. This eliminated the weekly bye. Hendry became captain of Richmond in place of Keating, Ransford captained Melbourne in place of Hendry, Morton captained South Melbourne in place of Park, whose medical career had reduced his spare time, and Jack Ellis led Prahran in place of Carl Willis who had shifted to the country.

Ponsford, again skipper of St Kilda, opened the season with 29 against Prahran and 55 against Melbourne. In the latter game he and Cohen put on 102 for the first wicket. A round of matches was played on Melbourne Cup Day and, while Nightmarch comfortably won the Cup from Paquito and the brilliant three-year-old Phar Lap, St Kilda and North Melbourne were involved in a dead-heat. Each side scored 86 runs. Ponsford's contribution was six. Woodfull, who had to that stage batted only once for 28 against Northcote, did not get a hand as the Prahran versus Carlton game was abandoned due to wet weather.

On the following Saturday, Woodfull made the most of his innings against the Colts and, in 191 minutes, hit a chanceless 132 not out. Ponsford was also unbeaten that day with 83 not out against Collingwood. In their next club appearances, after Victoria had played the MCC, Woodfull made 127 not out[3] in 227 minutes (the entire afternoon's play) against Melbourne, while Ponsford hit 85 against Richmond. He and Reg Ellis, who scored 192, added 203 for the second wicket.

The match against the MCC resulted in a seven-wicket win to Victoria, due chiefly to a second innings century by Woodfull and some fine bowling by Blackie. Ponsford had a poor game, scoring five and a duck and Woodfull's first innings duck was another reason Victoria failed by 71 to match the MCC's score. Blackie brought the State back into the game with a return of seven for 25 and the MCC collapsed to be all out for 114.

Needing 186 to win, Victoria overcame the early loss of Ponsford by the virtue of Woodfull's steady batting. Rigg joined him at the fall of the third wicket and with the score at three for 183 Rigg, who had made 39 with five fours, decided he would score no more. It was a sporting gesture as Woodfull was on 96 and a boundary would complete his century. Facing the last ball of an over from Barratt, which the bowler obligingly delivered underarm, Woodfull played a drive through the field. Rain had started to fall, so the fieldsmen headed for the pavilion on the assumption that the ball would reach the fence. Woodfull and Rigg started to follow, but when they noticed the ball stop short they returned to the crease and ran four. Woodfull's innings contained only four fours, but he reached his hundred in the reasonably brisk time of 164 minutes.

With the 1930 tour of England not very distant, a Test trial was played at the SCG between Woodfull's XI and Ryder's XI. Ponsford played with Ryder's team and was associated with Jackson in an opening stand worth 278. Jackson was in devastating form, hitting 182 in 187 minutes and overshadowing his more experienced partner. His dashing display included 27 fours and a six. Ponsford's innings of 131 included some grim defence — at one stage he didn't score for 20 minutes — but at other times he scored freely. He was at the crease for 242 minutes, hitting 10 fours and a six. Thanks to the two century-makers, Ryder's XI was four for 433 at stumps.

When eventually all out for 663, Ryder's XI then felt the full impact of the 21-year-old batting phenomenon named Bradman. After Woodfull had been dismissed for 36, Bradman was 54 not out at stumps on the second day. When play resumed he increased his score to 124, but, as Woodfull's XI totalled only 309, Bradman found himself batting again later in the day. This time he flayed the bowling to reach 205 by stumps in a score of two for 341. In less than a day's batting Bradman had hit 275.

The following day Bradman was out for 225 and Kippax hit a timely 170. Grimmett toiled away to finish with seven for 170 in the Woodfull XI's total of 541. Ryder kept himself and Ponsford back in the batting order, feeling they wouldn't be needed with less than 200 runs required to win. However, late in the day they were fighting to avoid defeat. At stumps Ryder's XI was eight for 152, needing 35 on the last day to win.

Ponsford (8) and Ryder (9) resumed and gradually picked up the necessary runs. With five still required Ponsford was out for 25. Grimmett, the last man in, survived and Ryder's XI won a memorable game by one wicket.

Victoria's first Sheffield Shield game for the season was against Queensland at the MCG and resulted in a five-wicket win for the home side, but a serious injury to Woodfull took the gloss off the game. 'Woody' had scored two in Victoria's first innings when he was hit on his left hand by a ball from 'Pud' Thurlow. Two bones were broken, forcing Woodfull to look on until the pre–1930 tour matches.

Ponsford made 28 and three against Queensland in a low-scoring game, but top-scored with 65 in a Victorian total of 229 against New South Wales. Trailing by 173 on the first innings, Victoria managed to force a draw by making 343 in its second knock. Ponsford managed only 12. 'Ponny' ran into better form against South Australia at the MCG making 47 and 110. He scored 54 in Adelaide but otherwise lacked the sparkle to which the game's followers had become accustomed.

At the end of January 1930 the team to tour England was selected and naturally Ponsford and Woodfull were in the party. To the surprise of most people Woodfull was named captain to succeed Ryder, who missed selection. It was generally accepted that Woodfull would one day lead Australia, but not in 1930 when Ryder was still playing well. Ryder's omission from the Australian team was variously described as a surprise, staggering, an insult, a tragedy and a move which left Victorians dumbfounded. From England, 'Plum' Warner commented that he thought Woodfull would be a capable and much-liked captain.

NOTES

[1]Brought to Sydney by his parents while still a child, Jackson began playing cricket at Balmain Primary School and by 15 had won a permanent place in the Balmain first XI. At 17 he made his debut with New South Wales. Tragically his Test career embraced only eight games and he died of tuberculosis early in 1933 at the age of 23. Ponsford and Woodfull were among the pall bearers at his funeral at the Field of Mars Cemetery.

[2]On the site of today's Southern Stand, taking up approximately the area of bays seven, eight and nine.

[3]Woodfull headed the 1929–30 VCA averages with 287.00 from three innings.

A NEW STAR

BY the time the Australian tourists journeyed to Tasmania for two matches in preparation for the 1930 tour of England, Ponsford's world record score of 437 had fallen to Bradman. The new batting star, destined to be even more prolific than the robust Victorian, had eclipsed the seemingly safe record by making 452 not out against Queensland in Sydney early in 1930. Bradman was on 80 when a ball from medium-pacer Alec Hurwood hit the wicket but did not dislodge the bails. His massive score took only 415 minutes and included 49 fours.

Hobart cricket followers had the honor of seeing the two heavy scorers bat together for the first time. Each hit a century and together they added 296 for the second wicket, Ponsford being slightly quicker in gathering his runs. Both batsmen were out at the same total, Ponsford having scored 166 and Bradman 139. Most notable batting by a Tasmanian came from Laurie Nash, who hit 93 in Tasmania's second innings score of five for 174[1].

The Australian XI game in Launceston was highlighted by 107 from 19-year-old New South Wales batsman Stan McCabe, who had not previously made a first-class century. Woodfull made 50 and Ponsford 36 in a total of 316.

A farewell luncheon was given to the tourists at the Hotel Alexander (later the Savoy) in Spencer Street, Melbourne, before the party left for Perth. Among the guests at the luncheon was Robert Menzies, at that stage a 35-year-old State parliamentarian who represented Nunawading in the Legislative Assembly. Addressing the gathering he eulogised Woodfull as one of the most outstanding cricketers of modern times. He had known Australia's new captain for many years and considered that his sole fault was that he had not dabbled in politics, which would have given him rudeness. Menzies said that he and the Premier (Ned Hogan) would be prepared to impart the necessary training.

Woodfull said the team would do its very best to bring back the Ashes and referred to his team as a body of young gentlemen who would assuredly play the game in the highest traditions of Australian cricket.

After a game in Perth, which the Australian XI won by an innings and 25 runs, the tourists sailed for England on the *Oronsay*.

Bradman and Woodfull dominated the batting in the opening first-class game of the tour against Worcestershire. Woodfull and Jackson opened after the country had been dismissed for 131 and apart from Fred Root, who was bowling to a leg-side field, the Australians had little to worry about. Jackson was out for 24 and then Woodfull and Bradman added 208 for the second wicket, which was broken when 'Woody' was bowled for 133 when trying to force the pace. He had hit 11 fours and a five during his 190-minute innings. Bradman finished with 236 in a score of eight for 492 (dec.). Worcestershire was all out for 196 in its second innings, giving the tourists a comfortable win and plenty of confidence for the games ahead.

Woodfull followed up his good form with 121 against Somerset, but it took Ponsford until his fifth innings to make a big score. Playing the MCC at Lord's, 'Ponny' came in at number five after Woodfull (52) and Bradman (66) had shared a second-wicket stand worth 119. Although wickets fell at the other end, Ponsford stood firm and was unconquered on 82 when the innings ended at 285. The MCC replied with 258, of which K. S. Duleepsinhji hit 92. Grimmett failed to take a wicket in conceding 78 runs, but Alan Fairfax put in a claim for a place in the first Test with six for 58.

Ponsford again showed good touch in the following match, against Derbyshire, and relished his reinstatement as an opener with a strong 131. At times he batted aggressively, hitting 18 fours, and during his 210 minutes at the crease appeared much sounder than he had been on English pitches in 1926. Ponsford shared a first-wicket stand of 127 with Jackson and when Australia batted a second time he made 30 not out. Percy Hornibrook also played a major part in Australia's 10-wicket win by claiming six wickets in each Derbyshire innings.

Before rain washed out the match against Surrey at The Oval, Woodfull and Bradman had been involved in their fourth century partnership of the tour by adding 118 for the second wicket. Wood-full's patient innings of 50 contained only one four, while Bradman hit out for another double century. When the match was abandoned he was 252 not out in a total of five for 379.

Although the advent of Bradman's batting genius had taken away much attention from Ponsford's efforts, the Victorian still had the ability to gain recognition by playing an outstanding innings. The match against Oxford University provided an example of this. Wood-full won the toss and sent McCabe in with Ponsford to start the innings. At stumps Ponsford was still batting with 220 to his name in a score of two for 406. McCabe, who made 91, helped 'Ponny' add 172 for the first wicket and later Kippax (56 not out) was associated in an unfinished third-wicket partnership worth 149. The other bats-man dismissed during the day was Bradman for 32. Oxford's attack included Ian Peebles who later played 13 Tests for England.

Woodfull closed the Australian innings after the first day and in reply Oxford scored 124 in both its innings. Bradman was used as a bowler in the second innings, taking two for 19.

The match against Hampshire began on May 31 with Bradman only 46 runs short of becoming the first visiting batsman to score 1000 runs before the end of May. Lionel Tennyson won the toss and Hampshire batted first, thus reducing Bradman's chances of batting on the first day. Grimmett helped his cause by taking seven for 39 in a score of 151 and Woodfull, keen to give Bradman the opportunity to get the runs, asked him to open the innings with Jackson. In the first over Jackson was out without scoring and Pons-ford replaced him. By tea, Bradman had cautiously made his way to 28 but as the players left the field rain began to fall heavily and did not stop until much later in the afternoon.

It seemed Bradman's assault on the 1000 runs had been washed away, but eventually play resumed and the Australian pushed his score to 35. Then the rain again fell, but Tennyson sportingly decided to play on for another over and the bowler, Norman, obliged with a couple of loose deliveries which Bradman hit to the boundary. Once he had reached 1000 runs for the tour, play stopped for the day. On the second day he carried his score to 191 out of his team's 334. Ponsford made 29 and Woodfull four. Grimmett also had a memorable game, taking a further seven wickets in Hampshire's second innings.

Ponsford was out cheaply in both innings against Middlesex — bowled middle stump by Nigel Haig in the second innings — and again against Cambridge University. On the other hand, Woodfull batted for six hours at Cambridge, making 216, including 20 fours. His role was that of a captain concentrating on building a big innings around himself. With the first Test the next engagement, it was a sensible idea. McCabe won himself Test selection for the first time, displacing Jackson, by making 96 at Cambridge.

Back in Ponsford and Woodfull's home city, Melburnians keenly awaited the arrival of Amy Johnson at Moonee Valley racecourse after she had become the first woman to fly solo from England to Australia. The previous year pioneer aviators Charles Kingsford-Smith and Charles Ulm had formed the first Australian National Airways, and started services between State capitals.

While the Empire shared the excitement of further progress in aviation, the first Test of the 1930s series began at Trent Bridge. For Woodfull it was not an auspicious start. He made only two and four and England won the match by 93 runs. It was to be his only loss for the series. It should be noted that Australia had shown considerable improvement as the 1928–29 Ashes series had progressed and England had reached the stage where some of its stars were past their prime.

England, eight for 241 at stumps on the first day, was all out for 270, due largely to its uncertainty against the spin of Grimmett who took five for 107 from 32 overs. The loss of Woodfull, Ponsford and Bradman to the bowling of Tate with only 16 scored made it hard for Australia to build a reasonable total and only Kippax (64 not out) and Vic Richardson (37) made any impression.

Australia was all out for 144 and England reinforced its advantage with a 125-run start from Hobbs and Sutcliffe. This partnership formed the base of a second innings total of 302. This left Australia needing a formidable 429 to win and at one stage, with Bradman batting so well, it seemed the goal might have been achieved.

At lunch on the fourth and final day Australia was three for 198 with Bradman and McCabe wanting 231 in the remaining 240 minutes. It was a tall order on a wearing pitch, but the New South Wales pair had pushed the score to 229 when McCabe fell to a great catch by substitute fieldsman S. H. Copley, a Nottinghamshire second XI player. It was something of a fairy-tale day for Copley, who thought someone was playing a joke on him when he received a telegram that morning asking him to be at the Trent Bridge ground to field in place of Larwood. Copley obeyed the instructions and played an important part in removing McCabe for 49.

The loss of Bradman and McCabe swung the game England's way although Australia's second innings total of 335 was far from disgraceful. Grimmett's 10-wicket haul — five in each innings — was also a satisfactory performance and one he followed up by taking six for 24 against Surrey. Woodfull excelled in the same match with an innings of 141. Ponsford did not bat between the first and second Test.

Described by the eminent writer Neville Cardus as the 'ideal Test', Australia won the second Test at Lord's by seven wickets. Although limited to four days, 1601 runs were scored and the game ended with an hour to spare. The game began with England in the ascendancy, being nine for 405 at the end of the first day. As delightful as its batting had been, however, the best was yet to come. Australia replied to England's 425, in which Duleepsinhji dominated with 173, by reaching two for 404 at stumps on the second day.

Ponsford and Woodfull were at their best, providing a brisk 162 in 175 minutes for the first wicket. Ponsford, who hit 81, was first to go and this was due indirectly to a visit from King George V. The teams were presented to His Majesty and on resumption 'Ponny' was caught off White's bowling. Bradman joined Woodfull, who batted more aggressively than usual, and the pair thrashed the bowling, adding 231 for the second wicket. Woodfull was stumped by Duckworth off Walter Robins shortly before stumps for 155.

Australia went on to make six for 729 before Woodfull declared. The score easily beat the previous highest for a Test innings which was England's 636 in Australia in 1928–29[2]. Apart from Woodfull and Ponsford, Bradman made 254 and Kippax 83. The historic scoreboard read:

W. M. WOODFULL, stpd. Duckworth, b Robins	155
W. H. PONSFORD, c Hammond, b White	81
D. G. BRADMAN, c Chapman, b White	254
A. F. KIPPAX, b White	83
S. J. McCABE, c Woolley, b Hammond	44
V. Y. RICHARDSON, c Hobbs, b Tate	30
W. A. OLDFIELD, not out	43
A. G. FAIRFAX, not out	20
Sundries,	19
Total for six wickets (dec.)	729

BOWLING

	Overs	Maidens	Runs	Wickets
Allen	34	7	115	0
Tate	64	16	148	1
White	51	7	158	3

Robins	42	1	172	1
Hammond	35	8	82	1
Woolley	6	0	35	0

England made a useful 375 in its second innings, Chapman leading the way with 121 and Allen lending strong suppport with 57, but it wasn't enough. Australia had ample time to score only 72 to wrap up the game. Yet the game took another turn when three of the greatest batsmen, Ponsford, Bradman and Kippax, were back in the pavilion with only 22 scored.

'Against Tate and Hammond, Ponsford batted as though intent on getting all the runs himself,' wrote Cardus. Ponsford was first out, for 14, followed by Bradman (1) and Kippax (3). McCabe joined Woodfull and the pair hit off the remaining 50 for victory.

Australia immediately made another shaky start, against Yorkshire at Bradford, when Woodfull and Bradman were out cheaply with only 17 runs scored. McCabe joined Ponsford and made a rapid 40 and then Jackson contributed 46 in a century stand. Ponsford went on to make a timely 143, almost half of his team's 302 and almost as many as Yorkshire's totals of 146 and 161. Grimmett, who had taken 10 for 37 in an innings when the Australians played Yorkshire at Sheffield earlier in the tour, had hauls of six for 75 and five for 58. Despite a 10-wicket win there were complaints from members of the Australian team, who were physically and mentally tired, when forced to play a strong country side immediately after a Test.

In the only other game before the third Test, Nottinghamshire proved hard to dislodge, making 433 in reply to the tourists' 296. Ponsford, bowled by Larwood for six, made 27 in a second innings tally of four for 360.

Ponsford missed the third Test at Headingley, Leeds, because of gastric trouble and Jackson opened in his place. Jackson was out for one in the opening over, which meant Bradman came in to face the new ball. He made light of the situation and by lunch had scored a century. At the other end Woodfull played a secondary but valuable role and when bowled by Hammond for 50 he had helped Bradman add 192 in yet another of their large second-wicket stands. Kippax, who hit 77, helped Bradman add 229 for the third wicket. By stumps Bradman was 309, having scored 105, 115 and 89 respectively in the day's three sessions.

Bradman, who had become the first player to score 300 in a Test innings in England, passed Sandham's recently established Test

The 1930 Australian tourists who brought home the Ashes. Back row (left to right) W.L. Kelly (manager), Archie Jackson, 'Tim' Wall, Ted a'Beckett, Percy Hornibrook, Alec Hurwood, Clarrie Grimmett, T. Howard (treasurer).
Front row (left to right) Alan Fairfax, Bill Ponsford, Vic Richardson (vice captain), Bill Woodfull (captain), Alan Kippax, Don Bradman, Charlie Walker.
Seated: Stan McCabe, Bert Oldfield.

Australian players at Joseph Rodgers & Sons, cutlery manufacturers, in Sheffield, Yorkshire, during the 1930 tour of England.

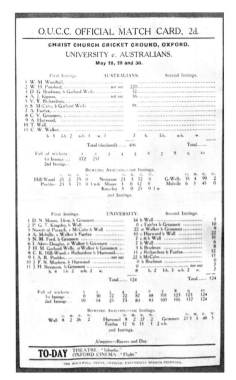

A scorecard printed after the tourists had played Oxford University in 1930. Ponsford dominated the game with an unbeaten 220.

Australian players Alan Kippax, Bill Ponsford, Stan McCabe and Ted a'Beckett with their host during a visit to Scotland in 1930.

record of 325 when he carried his score to 334 the next day. Bradman's huge score dominated the Australian innings of 566 and England did well to answer with 391. Hammond, whose four innings in the series had yielded only 82, found his true form and made 113. Chapman was next best with 45 but most of the Englishmen contributed. A draw was uppermost in their minds. At the finish, England was three for 95 after following on.

After a visit to Scotland, Australia went into the fourth Test at Old Trafford, Manchester, with Ponsford back in the side and Jackson out. Woodfull, driving powerfully, outscored his partner in a first-wicket stand of 106 in 150 minutes. Woodfull was first out, caught at the wicket off Tate for 54. Ponsford went on to make a chanceless 83 in 230 minutes, being bowled by Hammond with a perfect length delivery which moved several inches and took the leg bail as the batsman tried to leg-glance. Earlier in his innings, Ponsford, at 25, had hit a ball from spinner Peebles to Chapman and thinking he was out had begun walking from the wicket. Chapman returned the ball to the bowler, shaking his head to indicate a bump ball.

Kippax (51), Grimmett (50) and Fairfax (49) also got among the runs, but the rest of the side was out cheaply and Australia had to be content with 345 after its most promising start. Heavy rain, by no means uncommon in Manchester, brought the game to an end with England on eight for 251.

In the lead-up to the fifth Test, Ponsford scored a useful double of 53 and 35 not out in a drawn game against Glamorgan, and Woodfull hit a timely century against Northamptonshire, when the tourists suffered the indignity of having to follow on. In the latter match the Australians were all out for 93 in reply to the County's 249, off-spinner Jupp doing the damage with six for 32 from 23.4 overs. Bradman had managed 22 and Woodfull 15. Following on, Woodfull was 33 not out in a total of one for 96 at stumps on the second day. After the third and final day's play, the score stood at eight for 405 thanks to Woodfull and Richardson who both made 116. The South Australian hit 17 fours and a six, while Woodfull played a more restrained innings with only three fours.

Australia had to win the fifth and final Test at The Oval to win back the Ashes, held by England since 1926. With the series balanced at one win each and two draws, the match was scheduled to be played to a finish. England began the Test with a sound 405, built around an innings of 161 by Sutcliffe. Australia replied with a far more impressive performance.

Ponsford was in particularly fine touch and, despite a life at 45 when Duckworth spilled a chance, he reached 50 in only 65 minutes. When the century partnership with Woodfull was reached, Ponsford had made 75. 'Ponny' completed his own hundred in 135 minutes, at which stage Woodfull was 33, and was bowled by Peebles for 110 in failing light. The bowler had delivered a high ball, and the flight had deceived Ponsford because of a black cloud in the background.

The opening partnership was worth 159 and had blunted the England attack headed by Larwood and Tate. Bradman relished the position and helped himself to 232 although Larwood later claimed that 'the Don' was uncomfortable against faster, rising balls in line with the body. Bradman has disclaimed this and his score speaks for itself. Meanwhile, Woodfull had been dismissed for a valuable 54 and Jackson, McCabe and Fairfax all completed half centuries to send the Australian total soaring to 695.

England failed to make Australia bat again, losing Hobbs for nine in his farewell Test innings[3] and later succumbing to the spin of Hornibrook whose seven for 92 from 31.2 overs restricted the home team to 251. This left Australia a handsome winner by an innings and 39 runs. It also meant that the new skipper would take home the Ashes.

Woodfull (57.50) and Ponsford (55.00) each had a most successful Test series, as their averages indicate, but Bradman's abnormally high average of 139.14 overshadowed all aspects of the season.

A further five first-class games were played after the fifth Test, but the efforts of the two Victorian openers were minor compared with their earlier accomplishments on the tour. One significant game in which Ponsford played was the tie against Gloucestershire.

In a low-scoring game, the Australians replied to the county's first innings score of 72 with 157. Ponsford top-scored with an attractive 51 which included seven boundaries. Hammond made 89 in Gloucestershire's second innings total of 202, which left the tourists only 118 to win. Jackson and McCabe made exactly half of them, but then five wickets fell for 14 including Ponsford who was run out without scoring and it was left to the tailenders to restore order. Grimmett (12) and Hurwood (14) almost brought victory, but both were dismissed. Two runs were needed when wicketkeeper Charlie Walker joined Hornibrook. A single was scored to level the scores, then Hornibrook was bowled by off-spinner Tom Goddard who took seven for 54. The only other bowler used, Parker, took two for 54.

Ponsford's old adversary Tate had a good day when the Australians met Sussex at Hove. Tate bowled 'Ponny' for a duck and captured six for 82 in a total of 367 which was mostly due to Kippax's 158. Kippax followed with 102 not out in the second innings.

Ponsford's two ducks late in the tour were rarities for him and cost him a tour average of more than 50. Nevertheless his final figures of 1425 runs at 49.13 were most satisfactory and earned him fourth place on the tour averages. Woodfull was third with 1434 runs at 57.36. Kippax, helped by the Sussex game, ran second with 1451 runs at 58.04 and Bradman was an outright first with 2960 runs at 98.66.

Bradman's figures were phenomenal, but members of the touring party believed Woodfull's runs combined with his leadership constituted just as important a contribution. When the team arrived back in Australia, at Adelaide, a number of the players were openly indignant when Bradman flew on ahead of them and received a great reception in the major cities. That welcome, they believed, should have been given first to Woodfull.

Former England Test captain Pelham Warner, of whom more will be heard later, wrote glowingly of Woodfull's captaincy in his book *The Fight for the Ashes 1930:* 'I would go so far as to say that there has never been a more popular and better-liked Australian captain in this country. His characteristic walk, his charming smile, and his general manner and demeanor made him hosts of friends both on and off the field. It would be impossible, I should imagine, to have a nicer captain as one's vis-a-vis.

'In the field he was not such an outstanding personality as some earlier Australian captains, but he was a good one, quiet in his methods, sound in strategy and tactics, invariably manoeuvring his bowling well, and getting the best out of his side. He was the sort of captain for whom an eleven would do anything. Woodfull was also a capital speaker, who said what he had to say with sincerity and conviction, and who took his triumph in a modest and unassuming manner.'

NOTES

[1]Nash played two Tests, but was better known as a champion footballer with City (Launceston), South Melbourne and Camberwell.

[2]Later beaten by England with seven for 903 (dec.) against Australia in 1938. Australia exceeded its 1930 score with eight for 758 (dec.) against the West Indies in 1955.

[3]The Australian team lined up as Hobbs came to the wicket and Woodfull called for three cheers. Despite the emotion associated with such an occasion, Hobbs seemed unmoved and was playing smoothly when he tried to steer a short ball from Fairfax to third man but misjudged the movement off the pitch and played it on to his wicket.

FRESH OPPONENTS

THERE is no doubt that Jack Ryder was badly done by when he was dropped from the Australian team before the 1930 tour of England. Any resentment the 'King of Collingwood' might have had was well hidden and he remained a popular figure in the cricket world until his death in 1977 at age 87. The Victorian Cricket Association thought so highly of him that in 1930 it arranged a testimonial game at the MCG in mid-November, soon after Woodfull's tourists had arrived back from England.

Some indication of Ryder's standing with the Melbourne public can be gauged from the fact that a huge crowd of 44,434 attended the game on the Saturday. As a result of the well patronised game Ryder received a handout of £2463 ($4926) at a time when Australia was in the grip of an economic depression. Expressed in purchasing power, that amount of money was sufficient to buy a comfortable suburban home, fully furnished, with a brand new car in the garage.

On the Saturday night of the Ryder testimonial, a dinner was given at the MCG to welcome home Woodfull's team. Among the guests were the Minister for Railways, John Cain senior, Robert Menzies and the president of the Hawthorn-East Melbourne Cricket Club, Canon Hughes. Mr Cain presented Woodfull with an urn donated by a Tasmanian firm and inscribed by the Tasmanian Cricket Association (TCA). Ivor Evans, on behalf of the Australian Board of Control, presented Grimmett with the ball he had used to take all 10 Yorkshire wickets in an innings.

The Ryder testimonial, which was played between Woodfull's XI and Ryder's XI, was a forgettable match for Ponsford who was out for 14 and zero, while Woodfull made 53 and 13 not out. Jackson, who opened with Ponsford for Woodfull's XI, scored four and five. Ryder made an unbeaten 65 in his team's second innings, but loss of the third day because of rain caused the game to be drawn.

Major cricket and its principal players were taking on a new dimension, especially in the main Australian cities, because of the economic hardships most people were suffering. A Test match meant a great deal to many people, particularly those without work, because they were looking for things to do and outlets that would get their minds off the troubled times. Admission to games was relatively cheap, even if one had to put aside part of the weekly sustenance (dole) payment to save for the big occasion, and those who could least afford the tram or train fare generally lived within walking distance of the MCG or SCG. The inner suburbs of the big cities, such as Richmond and Collingwod in Melbourne and Redfern and Surry Hills in Sydney, were hardest hit by the Depression. A day at the cricket for an unemployed worker was a much-needed tonic.

Apart from the entertainment they provided, the players achieved the status of national heroes. For many, the feats of Ponsford, Woodfull and Bradman were talking points that were an endless source of satisfaction. It was certainly better than getting involved in a political discussion, which, in 1930, generally led to dissatisfaction.

In an era when a honeymoon was spent at Katoomba in New South Wales or Warburton in Victoria, when talking pictures were still a novelty and the California bungalow was a popular style of house, a big percentage of Australians identified with the Test cricketers of the day. By the end of 1930 Bradman was Australia's hero after his thrilling batting in England. His only rival was the four-legged champion of the turf, Phar Lap. Despite the acclaim Bradman received, and with justification, Ponsford was still highly regarded and Woodfull had won tremendous popularity through his leadership.

Meanwhile, a new set of rivals had arrived in Australia to challenge the might of world cricket. Led by George 'Jackie' Grant, the West Indies were new to the Test scene and many years were to lapse before they became a Test force. The West Indies had not played Test cricket until 1928 when a team was sent to England for a three-Test series. England won all three by an innings, but in 1929–30 when England made a visit to the Caribbean the West Indies won the third Test to square the series. England won the second Test and the other two were drawn.

Melbourne crowds had the privilege of watching talented batsmen George Headley hit 131 out of a modest total of 212 when the West Indies played Victoria, but otherwise the game was dominated by Victorians. The West Indies scored an early break in Victoria's innings when Woodfull was out without scoring, only to see his partner Ponsford run into his best form.

Ponsford and Hendry (44) carried the score to 69 and then Ryder (65) helped 'Ponny' take the total to 192. Keith Rigg joined Ponsford, who had reached his century after batting 209 minutes, and the pair added 200 for the fourth wicket. With 100 behind him, Ponsford hit out and added a further 87 in the next 77 minutes before being dismissed. Rigg then took over from his more experienced team mate and went a step closer to Test selection with 126. Len Darling, also destined to represent Australia, made 83 and Hawthorn-East Melbourne wicketkeeper Ben Barnett, another of the State's younger stars, hit 58 to enable Victoria to total 598.

Batting a second time the West Indies batsmen, with the exception of Headley who made 34, caved in against the veteran Ironmonger whose eight for 31 restricted them to 128 and gave Victoria victory by an innings and 258 runs.

The West Indies gave a better display in the first Test, in Adelaide, before an undefeated partnership of 172 between Ponsford and Jackson in Australia's second innings gave the home team a 10-wicket win. The West Indies' initial Test innings against Australia yielded 296. By stumps Australia had exceeded that score by one run with five wickets standing. Ponsford and Jackson gave their side a handy start of 53, but the loss of Jackson for 31 and, soon after, Ponsford (24) and Bradman (four) cast a different light on the game. Kippax and McCabe averted any serious trouble by adding 182 for the fourth wicket in a spirited recovery. McCabe made 90 and Kippax went on to score 146. Woodfull was run out for six in an Australian total of 376.

In its second innings the West Indies compiled 249, which left Australia needing 170 to win the Test. Ponsford and Jackson went about their task with care and patience; they were still together when Australia's objective was reached. Ponsford was 92 not out and Jackson 70 not out in a score of no wicket for 172.

Ponsford played another unconquered innings when he next batted, against New South Wales in Melbourne at Christmas. Woodfull was out for three and Victorian batsmen came in and went out before they could do much to help swell the score. All except, of course, for Ponsford who hit a century despite the batting disarray around him and eventually carried his bat for 109 not out in a total of 185.

Before rain washed out the game, Jackson was on his way to emulating the Victorian champion with 52 not out in the New South Wales score of six for 97.

Sydney cricket devotees recognised the significance of Ponsford's innings and gave him generous applause when he went out to open Australia's first innings at the start of the second Test at the SCG. A contemporary writer said of the occasion: 'When play began the historic ground was bathed in glorious sunshine and the green sward, which was at its best after the recent rain, looked a picture.'

Australia lost Jackson for eight with the score at 12 and Ponsford was unusually slow in taking an hour to reach double figures. Bradman was out for 25 and at lunch Australia was two for 66, Ponsford having made a dour 22. Kippax was out for 10 soon after play resumed and, at three for 69, Australia badly needed a solid partnership.

Ponsford and McCabe, taking extra care against paceman Learie Constantine, gradually steadied the innings and 'Ponny' brought up his half century after 145 minutes with his first boundary. The pair had added 71 when McCabe was trapped lbw for 31 by slow bowler O. C. 'Tommy' Scott. Woodfull replaced McCabe and he and Ponsford batted for the rest of the day.

Woodfull, playing his first Test in Sydney as captain, took his time reaching double figures although by tea Australia's position looked safer at four for 185. After the break Ponsford scored very freely, doubling his score from 87 to 174 by stumps. At 113 he survived a chance when he drove a ball back to Lionel Birkett, but the bowler couldn't make the catch. Woodfull, not feeling 100 per cent, played sedately and was 58 not out at stumps. The pair had added 183 to lift Australia's total to a very handy four for 323.

There was no play on the second day because of rain, which explains why the bowlers had such a harvest of wickets on the third day. Woodfull was out without adding to his score and Ponsford made only nine more before being bowled by Scott for a match-winning 183. His innings had taken 348 minutes and included 11 fours. With the tailenders exposed to the bowling, Australia fell away to be all out for 369.

In reply the West Indies struggled, making only 107 and 90. Grimmett took four for 54 in the first innings and Hurwood four for 22 in the follow-on. This gave Australia victory by an innings and 172 runs.

It was a similar story in the third Test in Brisbane. Australia batted first after Woodfull had won the toss, only this time Ponsford didn't have to lead a recovery, and the West Indies made a poor response to Australia's batting to lose by an innings and 217 runs. The series had been decided already.

The West Indies should have done much better as Jackson was dismissed in the first over and Bradman was missed in slips by Birkett off Constantine when his score was four. Bradman made the most of the chance and was still there at stumps with 223 to his name. He and Ponsford, who also batted forcefully for 109, added 229 for the second wicket. Here were the two masters of prolific scoring batting in tandem. The West Indies felt the impact of the partnership, as well as a fine 84 from Kippax. At the end of the day Australia was three for 428.

Fortunately for the Caribbean team Bradman was out first thing on the second day and Woodfull, batting at number six, was dismissed for 17 despite a careful innings. Australia was all out for 558, a smaller total than had been expected when play resumed, but still too much for the West Indies, despite a valiant effort by Headley to emulate Bradman. In a total of 193, Headley made an unbeaten 102. It would have been expecting too much of him to repeat such batting in the second innings and in the follow-on he made 28 of his side's 148.

Neither Ponsford nor Woodfull played in Victoria's match against New South Wales in Sydney or Victoria's second game against the West Indies. Without them Victoria struggled to a draw against the tourists, who surely could have claimed a moral victory. Yet Victoria's escape was also a case of the West Indies failing to press home the benefit of Headley making 77 and 113 in innings of 495 and five for 238 (dec.), respectively. Victoria, which had made 325 in its first innings, was nine for 250 when E. Healy joined L. O. Cordner in its second innings but the visitors failed to dislodge them and they added 30 in an unbroken last-wicket partnership.

Grant made a good start to the fourth Test, at the MCG, winning the toss and choosing to bat. It was to no avail. The West Indies batsmen could not handle the bowling of Ironmonger whose seven for 23 wrapped up the innings for 99. Woodfull returned to his more familiar role as opener in place of Jackson and, after Ponsford had been stumped off Constantine for 24, helped Bradman add 156 for the second wicket. Woodfull was run out for 83 and Bradman went on to make 152. Obviously there had been a certain amount of sacrifice by Woodfull in allowing Jackson to replace him as opener in the earlier Tests but Woodfull was very particular about team interests having priority over personal glory.

At eight for 328 Woodfull closed the Australian innings and again the West Indies failed to cope with Ironmonger who added four for 46 to his first innings haul to finish the match with 11 for 69. Fairfax, who opened the bowling with Ironmonger, also did well with four for 31 and Grimmett, the only other bowler called on, took two for 10. All out for 107, the West Indies lost by an innings and 122 runs. The Test was finished in two days.

Before the fifth Test in Sydney, Ponsford and Woodfull played their second Shield game for the season. Despite the continued good form of Woodfull and Ironmonger, Victoria was denied success when South Australia began the game with a solid 439. Ironmonger captured seven wickets, although they cost him 135 runs and Albert Lonergan starred for the home team with his career best score of 159.

Woodfull did his best to lift Victoria beyond the South Australian total by contributing 177, but Victoria's tally of 369 fell short by 70. Ponsford made 16. In its second innings South Australia managed only 154 after Ironmonger had taken five for 60, but there was insufficient time for Victoria to score the 225 needed for victory. When the game finished the visiting State was four for 131, of which Ponsford made 23 and Woodfull was 27 not out.

Australia went into the fifth Test with the chance of winning the series five-nil as Armstrong's men had done in 1920–21 against England. With overwhelming wins in each of the first four Tests, Australia had the form to repeat the effort, but the West Indies took the initiative from the start.

Batting first, the West Indies set the pace with the brilliant Headley (105) and Frank Martin scoring centuries to reach a commanding two for 298 at stumps on the opening day. Martin remained 123 not out when Grant declared at six for 350 on the second day, after rain had delayed the start of play. Australia began its chase by losing Ponsford for seven and Woodfull for 22, struggling to five for 89 at stumps. It was left to Fairfax, a very useful all-rounder, to top the batting the next day with 54 out of a total of 224.

Grant closed the West Indies' second innings at five for 124 when a day's play was lost due to rain. This left Australia 251 to win. Woodfull (18) and Ponsford (28) gave their country a handy start of 49 before the rot set in. The openers were caught by the agile Constantine and worse followed when Bradman and Oldfield were both dismissed without scoring. Kippax made only 10 and at five for 65 Australia was all but beaten. McCabe and Fairfax made a valiant effort to rescue the side, adding 79 for the sixth wicket before the former was out for 44. Even with McCabe out, Australia still had a faint chance of getting the runs as long as Fairfax stood firm. Oxenham (14) and Grimmett (12) lent useful support and Ironmonger's four was at least above his average, but overall it wasn't good enough.

Fairfax remained 60 not out when the last wicket fell for 220, giving West Indian cricket a major break with its first win in a Test away from home.

Test and Victorian appearances restricted Ponsford and Woodfull to only a handful of club games. Woodfull, whose aggregate of 287 runs for once out had won him the VCA averages the previous season, averaged only 22 with his 66 runs for Carlton in 1930–31. Ponsford hit two centuries in four innings with St Kilda, compiling 303 runs at 75.75 but his team was beaten in its semi-final against South Melbourne.

St Kilda had entered the finals confident of success after Ponsford and Ironmonger had dominated the penultimate home-and-away game at Northcote. Ponsford, initially wary of Northcote paceman Percy Chivers, settled into some brilliant batting and apart from a chance at 117 played flawlessly for 148 out of a total of seven for 274 (dec.). Northcote had the worst of the pitch on the second day and the wily Ironmonger exploited it to rout the home side for 46 and 75, taking six for 17 and six for 28 in the process.

In the last match St Kilda didn't bat as rain washed out the first day and South Melbourne batted throughout the second day. The teams met again in a semi-final and in a low-scoring game South hit 155 in reply to St Kilda's 133. Aware that quick runs would give it the chance to win outright, St Kilda adopted this tactic while South used the leg theory to negate the batsmen's efforts.

The Age referred to South's leg attack, noting that Bob Lawson bowled well outside the batsmen's legs, saying: 'The bowlers concentrated on leg theory, with nearly all the fieldsmen on the on-side, and run-getting was not easy. Most of the batsmen lost their wickets in swinging at the leg deliveries.' Ponsford met the challenge by working the ball to the off-side when possible and impressed in gathering 31 of his side's nine for 108 (dec.) after making only four in the first innings.

South Melbourne had scored three for 44, needing 87 to win outright, before rain ended the game. South's first innings lead earned it a place in the final in which Fitzroy won its first VCA flag.

While the state of Australian cricket was healthy, the nation's economy was still decidedly ill and more than a quarter of the workforce was unemployed. A single man on the dole received seven shillings ($0.70) a week and a married man without a family 14 shillings ($1.40). Those with children received more, but life was a struggle not only for those out of work but for those who felt their turn might be next.

The basic wage and margins for skill were cut by 10 per cent in 1931 and, amid the nation's falling morale, a fascist group of right-wing fanatics known as the New Guard took root in Sydney. On the brighter side of life, you could still see top-class cricket and there were signs that progress hadn't stopped completely. In Sydney, the Harbour Bridge was nearing completion and, in Melbourne, the building of the State Electricity Commission headquarters in Flinders Street and the proposed new Manchester Unity skyscraper were signs of hope for the future.

In 1931–32, following the first visit to Australia by the West Indies, South Africa made its first tour to Australia for 21 years. Woodfull enjoyed a particularly good season, but Ponsford was well below his usual form, largely through his difficulty in handling South African paceman Neville Quinn. Not only did Quinn restrict him to fewer than 100 runs in four Tests, but he also upset his confidence. Whereas Ponsford had played either forward or back to fast bowling, Quinn induced him to shuffle across his wicket, leading to all sorts of trouble. Only twice in 15 first-class innings did 'Ponny' hit more than 50.

Ponsford began the season with a new club, Melbourne, and made 13 on debut against Hawthorn-East Melbourne at Glenferrie Oval. Perhaps it was a bad omen. Woodfull started by being caught off the first ball against Prahran, but that innings was not indicative of what was to follow. In the next game, against North Melbourne, he celebrated the birth of his second son, Bill, by scoring 133. When dismissed, Woodfull declared at one for 240, his partner A. Jinks being on 100 and the team well ahead of North's score.

Victoria's first engagement for the season was against the South Africans. The great Victorian opening pair got away to their customary sound start with a stand of 67 before Ponsford was out for 37. Victoria then lost wickets steadily, but 'Woody' batted on and had scored 121 when he was ninth out after 270 minutes at the crease. Victoria's moderate total of 282 was enough to win the game as the tourists replied with only 235 and then rain ruled out any chance of good batting.

On a wet pitch, Victoria lost Woodfull for a duck and Ponsford for four before struggling to 91 in its second innings. This left the South Africans only 138 in arrears, but under the circumstances even that was too much. The Springboks crumbled to be all out for 53, Ironmonger taking five for 21 after his first innings return of five for 87 and Lisle Nagel took three for eight.

South Australia won a close encounter with Victoria in Adelaide by 21 runs, despite a hand of 134 by Ponsford. Chasing the home team's first innings total of 317, Victoria got within two runs. In the second innings its 151 fell short by 19. Woodfull's contributions were 32 and 19, while Ponsford failed to score in his second knock. So it was on to Brisbane for the first Test with both the Victorian openers having made a first-class century in the short lead-up.

Bradman and Woodfull set a pattern in the first Test of the 1931–32 series against South Africa that was to earn them more than half the runs scored by Australia. Bradman began his assault on the South African bowling with 226 and shared a second-wicket partnership of 163 with Woodfull, whose 76 was a most useful innings.

Woodfull had won the toss and in the first 15 minutes he and Ponsford had scored 19 runs. Quinn steadied the onslaught, but it was 'Sandy' Bell who broke through when he had Ponsford caught at first slip by Bruce Mitchell. It was the first of 23 wickets Bell was to take in the series. Considering he had only six innings in which to bowl and Bradman averaged 201.50, A. J. Bell did exceptionally well to gather so many wickets at a cost of only 27.3 each.

Ponsford, out for 19 in 41 minutes in a score of 32, was succeeded by Bradman who played steadily until lunch when the score was one for 74. After the interval he and Woodfull pushed along the run rate, Woodfull being trapped lbw by C. L. Vincent at 195. After Bradman had completed his double century, Oldfield hit 56 not out to help Australia reach 450.

South Africa made 170 and 117 in reply, the match being interrupted for several days by rain. Ironmonger finished with match figures of nine for 86 and South Australian fast bowler Thomas 'Tim' Wall took five for 14 in the second innings.

The second Test, in Sydney, produced a similar result although South Africa had the advantage of batting first. McCabe and Grimmett each took four wickets at little cost, restricting the Springboks to 153. Australia in reply lost Ponsford for five, but Woodfull made 58 and, with talented Victorian right-hander Keith Rigg, added 137 for the second wicket. Rigg, who had been twelfth man in the first Test, also had a third-wicket stand of 111 with Bradman. Rigg finished with 127, which was to remain his sole Test century, while Bradman made 112 and McCabe 79 in an Australian total of 469. South Africa made 161 in its second innings, leaving Australia the winner by an innings and 155 runs.

A second innings knock of 147 by Woodfull enabled Victoria to beat New South Wales by three wickets in the Christmas game at the MCG. The Victorians did well to score seven for 430 in the fourth innings of the game.

Ponsford, who made only six and five, had a similar fate when the third Test began at the MCG. This time he was bowled by Bell for seven. Bradman was out for two soon after and Woodfull, who lasted 48 minutes, also left for seven. At three for 25 Australia was in a shaky position. Kippax and Rigg each hit a half century, but the home team struggled all the way for its 198. South Africa replied with a very handy 358.

Australia was by no means beaten, but it required a big improvement in the second innings. Ponsford and Woodfull gave the side a sound start of 54 before the former, on 34, was caught one-handed in slips by Mitchell off Bell's bowling. This remained Ponsford's best innings of the series.

Woodfull was joined by Bradman and by stumps on the third day they had carried the score to one for 206, which put Australia back in the game. Five minutes before lunch on the next day Bradman was out for 167 when he was trapped lbw by Vincent. The second-wicket partnership had been worth 274, scored in only 183 minutes, and there was now a distinct chance that Australia could win the Test and the series.

At lunch Woodfull was 116 and he extended his chanceless innings to 161 before being caught by Mitchell off the bowling of McMillan with the total on 409. The Australian captain had batted for five hours in a painstaking display that had taken the initiative away from South Africa and placed the home team in a strong position. Kippax, who hit 67, and McCabe (71) carried on the good work of Woodfull and Bradman and as a result Australia reached an imposing total of 554.

South Africa, needing 395 to win, found the target too great, especially when Woodfull had a spinner such as Grimmett to do the bulk of the bowling. Grimmett captured six for 92 to spin out the Springboks for 225 and give Australia a 169-run win.

Neither of the Australian openers played for Victoria against New South Wales in Sydney, a match which ended shortly before the fourth Test in Adelaide. Woodfull enjoyed further success, both with the bat and as captain, but Ponsford again fell cheaply in the first innings. Fortunately for Australia Ponsford's failure didn't affect the rest of the batting because Woodfull and Bradman were in such great form. Nevertheless, the cricket-loving public was disappointed that a batsman of Ponsford's standing could not 'click'.

Despite the persistence of Grimmett, who took seven for 116, South Africa began the fourth Test with a respectable total of 308. In reply, Australia lost Ponsford at nine, when he was bowled by Quinn for five. The Springboks were elated, but their early success receded as Woodfull and Bradman began another big partnership for the second wicket. This time they put on 176 before 'Woody' was out for 82. Bradman went on to make an unbeaten 299 in a total of 513. With his score on 298 Bradman beat the field and seemed set for another triple Test century. After taking the first run, Bradman realised that a second would be risky and tried to stop his partner, Queenslander Hugh Thurlow, from continuing. He was too late; a smart return from Ken Viljoen ran Thurlow out before he could regain his crease.

Grimmett added to his fine record by taking seven for 83 in South Africa's second innings of 274 and opened the way to a 10-wicket win. In Australia's second innings of none for 73 Woodfull was 37 not out and Ponsford 27 not out when the game finished.

As a lead-up to the fifth Test, Victoria played South Africa for the second time. The highlight of a rain-interrupted game was an unfinished first-wicket stand of 158 between Ponsford and Woodfull in Victoria's second innings. Ponsford, out for eight in the first innings, made 84 not out and Woodfull 73 not out. South Africa had led Victoria 239 runs to 231 in the first innings, but the drawn game was of little value except that it helped Ponsford regain his confidence. Unfortunately he was unable to take his restored form into the fifth Test at the MCG because an attack of influenza forced him to miss the game. Rigg opened the batting in his place.

Due to a soft, wet pitch the match was an exceptionally low-scoring one, as South Africa's first innings total of 36 indicates. Ironmonger took five for six and Nash, playing in his first Test, took four for 18. Australia also struggled to make runs although its tally of 153 turned out to be a satisfactory effort. Another Test newcomer, Jack Fingleton, showed promise by making 40 as an opener. Rigg scored a useful 22 and Kippax top-scored with 42. Woodfull failed to score.

South Africa's second innings was another disaster. Nash caught and bowled Christy before a run was scored and after Curnow showed some resistance in compiling 16, wickets tumbled like ninepins. From three for 30 the Springboks collapsed to nine for 33 before Quinn and Vincent carried the score to 45. Ironmonger's haul of six for 18 gave him the staggering figures of 11 for 24 for the match and 31 wickets in the series at a cost of 9.54 runs each. O'Reilly snared three for 19 and Nash one for 4. The fascinating point about this Test is that Grimmett did not get a bowl after taking 33 wickets at 16.83 apiece in the first four Tests.

Woodfull had joined Warwick Armstrong in leading Australia to a clean sweep in a five-Test series and with Bradman had scored more than half the runs made by Australia in the series. Bradman made a total of 806 and Woodfull 421.

Ponsford was out cheaply in both innings when Melbourne lost to St Kilda in a VCA semi-final, but an innings of 161 not out against Carlton[1] earlier in the season enabled him to score 269 runs at an average of 53.80 for his new club. This left him in eighth place in the association averages. Woodfull, with 213 runs at 53.25, was ninth.

On April 1 1932 Ponsford began a new job. After five years with the Melbourne *Herald* he joined the Melbourne Cricket Club staff as office manager. He remained with the MCC until he retired on Friday, June 13 1969, having served under three secretaries: Hugh Trumble, Vernon Ransford and Ian Johnson.

NOTES

[1]Ponsford and Len Darling gave Melbourne a start of 180 before Darling was out for 104. Ponsford batted for 236 minutes for his unbeaten 161 in a total of eight for 373. He hit 11 fours and didn't give a chance until he was 154. On the same afternoon three other batsmen made centuries in the round of District matches. They were Haydn Bunton, who hit 104 for Fitzroy against Prahran; Hawthorn-East Melbourne veteran Lou Salvana, who made 111 against University; and Lindsay Hassett, a promising 18-year-old who hit 111 for South Melbourne against Collingwood.

BODYLINE

NGLAND realised before it embarked on the 1932–33 tour of Australia that the batting brilliance of Bradman was enough to enable Australia to retain the Ashes. Pelham 'Plum' Warner, manager of the tourists, had written in his book *The Fight For The Ashes 1930:* 'It is a disturbing thought that he (Bradman) is still only a boy. We must, if possible, develop fresh ideas on strategy and tactics to curb his almost uncanny skill.' In the space of only four Test series, Bradman, in 19 Tests, had already scored 2695 runs at the astonishing average of 112.29.

During the fifth Test at The Oval in 1930 an incident occurred that was to have a profound effect on the 1932–33 series. Bradman had made 175 when he received a very fast ball from Larwood which struck him under the heart. According to Warner, Bradman seemed inclined to draw away from Larwood for an over or two before regaining his confidence and playing some fine strokes to leg off the rising ball on his body.

Although it was only human for Bradman to be uncomfortable against Larwood's bowling immediately after being hurt, the English saw this as a weakness in his technique and decided that it could best be exploited by use of fast leg-theory. The plan that evolved was not merely a revival of a strategy that had been employed before, often with indifferent results, but a highly questionable, dangerous form of attack that exceeded the spirit of the game.

Leg-theory, in which the bowler attacked the leg stump with the

Ponsford picks up runs on the off-side during the fourth Test against England at Old Trafford in 1930. 'Ponny' top-scored with 83 and shared an opening stand of 106 with Woodfull, who hit 54.

Relaxing with a round of golf at West Kent during the 1930 tour of England are Bill Ponsford, Stan McCabe and Percy Hornibrook.

Arriving home after the 1930 tour, Ponsford is re-united with his wife Vera and son Bill.

Bill Ponsford's sons Geoff and Bill pictured with their mother.

support of an on-side field, had been used in both England and Australia for 50 years, possibly longer. As a rule it was a defensive way of bowling and did not win much favour from captains. Warner wrote in 1930 that 'It is a waste of time, a confession of weakness, and a negation of the science of bowling.'

Bodyline bowling, as it became known in Australia, was something different. It was executed by an express bowler and was aimed not at the leg stump but at the batsman himself. A ring of leg-side fieldsmen waited for the inevitable mis-hit. A typical bodyline field was comprised of three leg slips, a short square leg, a forward square leg and a silly mid-on. This inner ring was backed by a fine leg and, for hookers, an extra man was placed in the deep. Proponents of bodyline argued that the batsman wasn't being denied the chance to make a big score as long as he could hook safely. McCabe proved this when he hit an unconquered 187 in the first Test in Sydney, but generally speaking a batsman had first to protect himself, then to protect his wicket and then try to score runs.

The tactic was the responsibility of England captain Douglas Jardine, who adapted it from leg-theory after discussing it with various cricket identities including Larwood, Percy Fender, Arthur Carr and Bill Voce. The principals in the bodyline controversy were Jardine and Larwood with Voce, who opened the Nottinghamshire attack, playing a supporting role.

Jardine and Larwood made an interesting juxtaposition, especially in the light of the successful implementation of Jardine's nefarious plans to subdue Bradman. Jardine was born in Bombay on October 23 1900 (four days after Ponsford) to Alison and Malcolm Jardine. Malcolm Jardine, who was a lawyer, worked in India from 1894–1916. Douglas Jardine, his only child, was educated at Winchester and Oxford and eventually became a solicitor. He was a complex character whose aloofness and independence tended to antagonise rather than endear, especially with the Australian 'ocker'. Jardine played cricket with Oxford University and Surrey before making his Test debut against the West Indies at Lord's in 1928.

Strong defence was the basis of his batting, which was not attractive but was of immense value to his team. After 22 Tests he had a final batting average of 48, but, because he was so slow, his aggregate of 1296 runs contained only one century. Captain of England in 15 Tests, he is remembered for wearing a harlequin cap with blue, maroon and buff quarterings, a factor which irritated many cricket followers. Jardine is understood to have begun wearing the cap at the start of the 1928–29 tour of Australia in a mildly superstitious gesture to score more runs, rather than as an act of non-conformity.

Harold Larwood represented the antithesis of Jardine. Born at Nuncargate, Nottinghamshire on November 14 1904, he had little education and as a 14-year-old stripling was working as a coal-miner to help his family make ends meet. His father had captained the colliery cricket team and young Harold was still a teenager when Nottinghamshire county officials heard of his promise. Realising that making the grade as a professional cricketer meant a life out of doors rather than underground, Larwood worked towards his goal and it wasn't long before he graduated to the England team in 1926 at only 21. Although not big in stature, Larwood was strong and had the ability to get the ball to rise up to shoulder height from a perfect length. His run of almost 25 metres was rhythmic, with the left leg thrust forward like the driving wheel of a powerful steam locomotive. By the time he delivered the ball Larwood had worked up terrific momentum as he glided, rather than stormed, to the wicket. More than half a century after the bodyline series Ponsford, reflecting on the best bowlers he faced, was generous in his praise for Larwood because he could get the ball to rise sharply off a good length.

In 1932 Larwood had taken 162 wickets for Nottinghamshire at an average of only 12.86 runs per wicket to head the English first-class averages. Jardine was well aware that this man, more than any other bowler, could turn leg-theory into a lethal weapon. Possibly Jardine's thoughts had been reinforced by a match at Folkestone between an England XI and the Australians near the end of the 1926 tour. Three English players — Bob Wyatt, 'Tiger' Smith and Fred Calthorpe — were delayed by thunderstorms on their way from Woking and the match began with Herbie Collins and two other Australians fielding as substitutes for the England XI. Smith's place as wicketkeeper was temporarily taken by Jardine who had the rare experience of keeping to Larwood. The young Notts express had a day out, starting by having Woodfull caught in the covers by Collins (the Australian captain) for two and later bowling Ponsford around his legs for 47. Bardsley, Collins, Ryder, Hendry, and Oldfield also formed part of Larwood's impressive haul of seven for 95 which probably left its mark in more ways than one.

As a professional work-horse playing under an amateur captain, Larwood was hardly in a position to refuse Jardine's request to bowl bodyline. In fact, Larwood may have seen the chance to prove a point or two. For much of his career he had been unhappy that curators tended to prepare pitches that suited batsmen and offered fast bowlers little encouragement. As well, he had not forgotten the thrashing Bradman had dealt his bowling in 1930. Unlike George 'Gubby' Allen, who as an amateur, refused to bowl bodyline, Larwood was happy to oblige.

Meanwhile, Ponsford and Woodfull had made a sound start to the season in Sheffield Shield matches in Brisbane and Sydney. In view of his indifferent efforts the previous season, Ponsford's form was particularly pleasing. Against Queensland he and Woodfull, who made 35, had an opening stand worth 76 and against New South Wales the pair started with 138 before Woodfull was run out for 74 by a throw from Kippax. In the former game Ponsford went on to make 98 (run out) and in Sydney he made 200 of Victoria's first innings total of 404. Injury prevented 'Ponny' from batting in the second innings, but Woodfull hit 83 of the side's 150.

The English party, which by this stage had arrived in Australia, must have looked at the results of the New South Wales versus Victoria game with more than a passing interest. Despite the combined efforts of Ponsford and Woodfull, Victoria lost the game by nine wickets. Bradman, in scoring 238 and 52 not out, confirmed the worst fears held by his opponents that he was set for another fine season.

Victoria's first match against the MCC was played immediately after the Victorians returned from Sydney. Ponsford did not play because of a sprained ankle he sustained in the New South Wales game and Leo O'Brien, who had made 145 not out in Brisbane, was promoted in the batting order to open with Woodfull. Larwood was rested for this game, but his opening partner from Nottinghamshire, Bill Voce, played and gave some indication of what was to come by bowling aggressively to a leg-side field. It was not bodyline, which was to be first used against an Australian XI in the next game.

The tourists had no trouble beating Victoria, whose batting was poor. Woodfull was out for five and 25 and again had problems while captaining the Australian XI. The match, played in Melbourne, began on November 18 1932 and the visitors were all out for 282. With the prospect of seeing Bradman bat the next day, a Saturday, a huge crowd of 53,916 attended the MCG. O'Brien and Woodfull opened to some hostile bowling by Larwood and at one stage Woodfull was on the point of collapse when struck in the chest. After a brief delay Woodfull resumed batting, but with the total at 51 and his own score on 18 he was out lbw to Bowes.

Bradman entered the fray intent on meeting hostility with hostility. After taking 13 off an over from Bill Bowes he faced Larwood, brought on to replace Bowes, for the first time for the season. Bradman promptly cut a short ball to the boundary and, after evading a bouncer, hooked another short delivery to the fence. Bob Wyatt, deputising for Jardine who had taken time off to enjoy a spot of fishing, then switched his slips fieldsmen to leg and bodyline was on in earnest.

Bradman had reached 36 in only 45 minutes when he tried to turn Larwood to the on-side, missed and was given out lbw. Bradman seemed unruffled by the decision although it was later suggested he was most unlucky. The perturbing side to his brief innings was that he hadn't batted with the same authority that he showed under normal circumstances. Larwood later claimed a victory, saying that his tactics had rattled Bradman.

O'Brien's 46 was the top score in the Australian XI total of 218, while Larwood finished with four for 54. Medium pace bowler Lisle Nagel then routed the MCC for 60, taking a career best of eight for 32. Before the Australian XI began its second innings, rain halted play and in the time remaining scored two for 19. Both wickets fell to Larwood, including that of Woodfull for a duck.

As if the tactic of using bodyline bowling were not enough, the Australian Test team had another setback when it was announced that Bradman was unfit to play in the first Test in Sydney. For more than two years he had been under terrific pressure, both physically and mentally. Not only had he played a lot of cricket in that short time but he was so good that the public expected big things from him whenever he batted. By November 1932 he was suffering from nervous exhaustion and badly needed a rest.

Although Bradman was absent, bodyline was still used against the Australian batsmen. For a time it seemed the dashing McCabe had negated the tactic as he hooked, pulled and cut his way to an unbeaten 187. His masterly innings included 25 boundaries, but regrettably he was to play only one other big innings for the rest of the series. On the other hand, Kippax was unable to cope with bodyline and did not play Test cricket again that season.

Australia was in trouble soon after the first Test began, losing Woodfull for seven. Ponsford reached 32, but was bowled around his legs by Larwood who also removed Fingleton (26) and Kippax (8) in the same spell. McCabe and Richardson (49) steadied the Australian innings which might have reached a bigger total than 360 had the tailenders managed to hold out a little longer. Larwood finished with five for 96 and Voce four for 110, having bowled 60 overs between them.

The Australian effort was easily surpassed by England, whose total of 524 included three centuries. Opener Sutcliffe hit 194, the reliable Hammond made 112 and the Nawab of Pataudi justified his place at number four with 102.

England consolidated its position by mowing down the Australians for 164 in their second innings. Fingleton top-scored with 40 and McCabe followed his epic first innings with 32, but both Woodfull and Richardson failed to score and Ponsford was bowled by Voce for two. Larwood's five for 28 from 18 overs tells much of the story. England's second innings consisted of one ball, Sutcliffe scoring a single off McCabe to give the tourists a 10-wicket win.

Shortly before the second Test, in Melbourne, Victoria met New South Wales in the traditional Christmas game. In a rain-interrupted contest, New South Wales took first innings points. This was due largely to 157 from Bradman who exercised caution on his way to the century, but later scored at better than even-time. Obviously his rest had been beneficial and he was ready to resume Test play.

Ponsford, who scored 12 against New South Wales, was dropped for the second Test to make way for O'Brien, who had been batting consistently for Victoria. At the age of 25 he appeared to have a bright future. A sound batsmen against fast bowling, O'Brien was a left-hander and this fact probably influenced his selection as it was felt that leg-theory was less effective against left-handed batsmen.

Ironmonger also gained inclusion at Nagel's expense and Kippax was left out to make way for Bradman. Ponsford's omission meant that Fingleton moved from number three to open with Woodfull and O'Brien was used at the fall of the first wicket. A then world record cricket crowd of 63,993 packed the MCG[1] on the first day. It would be interesting to know how many people arrived after the start of play when it was known that Australia was batting, or to put it more bluntly, that Bradman would bat that day.

Fingleton, a 24-year-old journalist from Sydney's Waverley club, proved the mainstay of the Australian innings. A patient player who was well suited to opening an innings, Fingleton steadily gathered runs while both Woodfull and O'Brien were out for 10 and Bradman without scoring. The latter's dismissal left the crowd stunned. Given the welcome of a hero, Bradman faced Bowes for only one ball and, in most uncharacteristic style, dragged it from outside the off stump onto his leg stump. McCabe (32) and Richardson (34) lent useful support to Fingleton, whose 83 dominated an innings that amounted to only 228.

Against Wall and O'Reilly, England found runs even harder to come by and was all out for 169. Wall captured the wickets of Sutcliffe,

Hammond, Jardine and Ames for 52 runs, while O'Reilly took five for 63 off 34.3 overs.

The third day of the match was on Monday, January 2 1933 — the New Year's Day public holiday — and a fresh world record was established when a crowd of 68,188 gathered. Bradman was again the magnet and this time he thrilled his legion of admirers. After Woodfull had been caught in the leg trap off Larwood for 26, only Bradman (103 not out) and Richardson (32) succeeded in making any headway. Bradman was still two runs short of his century when last-man Ironmonger came to the crease. He survived long enough to enable 'The Don' to complete his century and was then run out without scoring.

Australia had made only 191, which left England 251 to win, but the spin of O'Reilly and Ironmonger routed the visitors for 139 to give Australia victory by 111 runs. O'Reilly, who started the collapse by removing Sutcliffe, Wyatt and Hammond, took five for 66. Ironmonger secured four for 26 from 19.1 overs.

At this stage the series was even with one win apiece, Larwood had captured 14 wickets and both Bradman and McCabe had scored a significant century. Bodyline had already had an effect on the Australian batting, but it remained to be seen whether the tactics would endure.

The nastiness of bodyline welled up into a bitter confrontation in Adelaide. The relationships between the opposing sides became so strained that Test matches between Australia and England faced extinction. Woodfull's level-headed approach to the crisis went a long way to saving the situation from degenerating into a fracas. Of the players with cause to become enraged, Woodfull was the first and he could have been excused for resorting to retaliation. That he didn't is to his eternal credit.

Australia reinstated Ponsford for this Test, relegating O'Brien to twelfth man, but used 'Ponny' at number five. England batted first after Jardine had won his only toss for the series. Four early wickets fell for only 30 runs, but Leyland (83), Wyatt (78) and Eddie Paynter (77) averted further trouble and later Hedley Verity contributed a valuable 45. England's score of 341 was a sound one, especially after such an insecure start.

The Australian innings began midway through the second day and immediately received a setback when Fingleton was dismissed by Allen, using orthodox methods, without scoring. Larwood was also bowling to an off-side field when he struck Woodfull a fearful blow above the heart with the last ball of his second over. The delivery was not a bouncer, but short-pitched and its impact caused Woodfull to drop his bat and stagger away from the wicket. Apart from hurting the Australian captain, the crowd of 50,962[2] was incensed by the incident.

Mrs Gwen Woodfull, at home in Melbourne, minding her young family wasn't too happy either and more than half a century after the incident was quick to comment that she believed that the injury was to blame for her husband's death. Mrs Woodfull was in constant touch during the match and was most concerned that the bodyline tactics could have serious consequences.

Woodfull did not leave the field after being hit and once he regained his composure, indicated that he was well enough to continue. Allen began a new over to Bradman and Woodfull remained at the non-striker's end for the over while Bradman scored a four and a two. This brought Woodfull face to face with Larwood again. Jardine switched the field to the leg-side in readiness for a bodyline attack. On the surface it was a most callous act although either Jardine or Larwood could have had Bradman in mind and overlooked the fact that Woodfull had just taken a physical battering. Nevertheless, Jardine could have waited until Bradman took strike before making the switch.

Whatever his intent, Jardine succeeded in dismissing Bradman cheaply. 'The Don' had made only eight when he was caught on the leg-side by Allen off Larwood. Woodfull reached 22 before being bowled by Allen and McCabe was caught off Larwood for eight. This left Ponsford and Richardson with the unenviable task of rebuilding the innings and by stumps the former was 45 not out in a total of four for 109.

While Ponsford was out in the middle of the field defying the England attack, Woodfull became involved in an unpleasant exchange with Warner in the Australian dressing rooms. Towards the end of play Warner and his co-manager, R.C.N. Palairet, decided to visit Woodfull to see how he was after his injury. Warner probably regarded it as a gesture of goodwill. Woodfull certainly didn't and reacted angrily when he saw the Englishmen: 'I don't want to see you, Mr Warner. There are two teams out there. One is trying to play cricket and the other is not.'

According to Leo O'Brien, the Australian twelfth man, Woodfull had just stepped out of a shower and was not on the massage table as has sometimes been suggested. 'Warner was the only one who spoke to Woodfull. Palairet just stood there,' O'Brien recalled.

Woodfull's rebuke of Warner, which he never withdrew, was the culmination of a nasty day but worse was to follow when play resumed on Monday. Ponsford continued to bat courageously, preferring to take a bouncer on his fleshy back rather than risk hitting a catch to the cluster of leg-side fieldsmen. He lifted his score to 85 and, with Oldfield, added 63 for the sixth-wicket. After Ponsford was bowled by Voce, Oldfield continued to bat well and the 200 was raised. Larwood took the new ball and bowled to an orthodox field, as was the custom before the shine came off the ball, but Oldfield was untroubled by the English speedster. Larwood then switched to the bodyline field and Oldfield, trying to hook a rising ball, snicked it on to his right temple.

Oldfield reeled towards slips and collapsed. Several England players ran to his assistance and Woodfull, dressed in a suit, hurried from the pavilion to the wicket. Oldfield, who had scored 41, made his own way from the field but took no further part in the game and was forced to miss the fourth Test.

The crowd was infuriated by the Oldfield incident and according to a future Broken Hill newspaper editor who was at the game, it would have taken only one person to lean across the arena fence to retrieve a dropped two shilling piece and the crowd would have invaded the ground. Had the incident taken place in Oldfield's home city of Sydney, who knows what the 'Hill mob' might have done?[3]

After Oldfield's enforced departure the Australian innings was wound up for 222, Allen's four for 71 being the best bowling figures. Richardson substituted for Oldfield behind the stumps in England's second innings in which six players scored 40 or more to lift the total to 412. This left Australia needing 532 to win and it wasn't long before the team was again struggling. Fingleton was bowled by Larwood for a duck — his second duck in the Test — and Ponsford, batting at number three, was caught off Larwood for three.

For the next 73 minutes Bradman dominated play, thrashing 66 off the bowlers in an unconventional but effective way of countering bodyline. Among the shots he played was a cut to a ball on the leg stump. At the other end Woodfull defied the attack with great courage and resource, eventually carrying his bat for 73 not out while the innings crumbled to a disappointing 193. This left England a decisive winner by 338 runs.

As a result of the incidents in the Adelaide Test, Woodfull complained to the Australian Board of Control and its secretary Bill Jeanes. The Board, in turn, cabled the MCC on Wednesday January 18, two days after Oldfield was hurt, stating that, 'Bodyline bowling has assumed such proportions as to menace the best interests of the game, making protection of the body by the batsmen the main consideration. This is causing intensely bitter feeling between the players, as well as injury. In our opinion, it is unsportsmanlike. Unless stopped at once, it is likely to upset the friendly relations between Australia and England.'

The Marylebone Cricket Club met the following Monday to reply to the Australian condemnation of the English tactics. As the blue bloods of the MCC awoke to a London winter's morn, Jardine was thanking the ladies of the Ballarat Croquet Club for their hospitality in providing afternoon tea for the English cricketers who were playing a Ballarat and district side.

The Ballarat game, played on the Saturday and Monday following the Adelaide Test, was calm by comparison. The local side was allowed to bat 13 players, although it was restricted to 11 fieldsmen, and was also permitted to reinforce the team with three players from Melbourne teams. They were fast bowler Harry 'Bull' Alexander (Essendon), batsman Ernie Bromley (St Kilda) and all-rounder Percy Beames (Melbourne). Beames, a former Ballarat resident who later represented Victoria at both cricket and football, recalled in 1984 that he had travelled to Ballarat by train with Bromley and Alexander and during the trip Alexander said that he had been told by the VCA not to use retaliatory bowling. Alexander, a thick-set player whose natural game was to bowl short and pound the ball into the turf, was regarded at the time as a possible retaliatory weapon against Larwood.

Larwood did not play in the Ballarat game, in which the tourists did not fraternise with the locals. 'They never spoke to us and Jardine acted in a very supercilious way on the field,' said Beames. The Ballarat captain, Bert Rogerson, recalled that when inclement weather halted play on the Monday and he and Jardine went to inspect the pitch, the England captain was more interested in asking him what Ballarat had to offer in the way of cinemas. The match, in which the provincial team scored eight for 84 in reply to the tourists' 255, was a rather pleasant interlude for Jardine and his men.

After leaving the City Oval and picking up their belongings from their hotel, the players assembled at Ballarat Railway Station to catch a train to Melbourne. Jardine strolled down to the eastern end of the platform where a locomotive in steam caught his attention. He looked at the engine with admiration while the fireman, recognising him, gathered a shovelful of cinders and called out: 'Hey, Mr Jardine, here are the ashes. Would you like to take them back to England with you?' Jardine tossed back his head arrogantly in a silent reply.

On the other side of the world the MCC didn't care for the Australian cable, especially the reference to unsportsmanlike behavior. They replied that it had the fullest confidence in the captain, team and managers and that they would do nothing to infringe the laws or the spirit of the game.

The Australian Board of Control sent a second cable, worded more diplomatically, but the charge of being unsportsmanlike was not dropped. Jardine's reaction was that if the word was not withdrawn there would be no fourth and fifth Test. Eventually, after diplomatic and prime ministerial intervention, the Board of Control, two days before the fourth Test, cabled the MCC saying: 'We do not regard the sportsmanship of your team as being in question. Our position was fully considered at the recent Sydney meeting, and is as indicated in our cable of January 30. It is the particular class of bowling referred to therein which we consider not in the best interests of cricket, and in this view we understand we are supported by many eminent English cricketers.'

Jardine accepted the statement although the issue of whether bodyline was unsportsmanlike had not been addressed.

The fourth Test, in Brisbane, went ahead and Larwood continued bowling bodyline. Voce missed the game because of injury. The Australian selectors dropped Fingleton and Grimmett for left-hand batsmen Len Darling and Bromley. Hampden Love replaced wicket-keeper Oldfield, injured in the third Test.

After winning the toss and batting, Woodfull was associated in an opening partnership of 133 with Richardson on a placid pitch of little benefit to bodyline bowling. It was Hammond who broke the stand, having Richardson stumped by Ames for 83. Woodfull, who was joined by Bradman, advanced to 67 before he was bowled by Derbyshire spinner Tom Mitchell. The only other batsman out on the first day was McCabe for 20, while Bradman ran into some good form after a scratchy start to be 71 in a total of three for 251 at stumps.

Given the form shown on the first day Australia was expecting a score of 400 or more, but early on the second day Larwood bowled both the overnight batsmen. Bradman was out for 76 and Ponsford 19. Later in the innings Larwood removed Bromley and O'Reilly to finish with four for 101 in Australia's total of 340. Jardine and Sutcliffe steered England to none for 99 by stumps. England's position deteriorated on the third day to the extent that half the side was out with less than 200 runs scored. To add to England's troubles, Lancashire batsman Eddie Paynter was in hospital with tonsilitis and a touch of sunstroke.

Paynter discharged himself from hospital and came to the crease at the fall of the sixth wicket. Despite his groggy condition he managed to make 24 by stumps and, after spending the night in hospital, completed a very useful innings of 83 the next day. His effort allowed England to reach 356, a lead of 16, and provided a big step toward victory, especially when Australia folded for 175 in its second innings. Ponsford, for the first and only time in a Test match, was out without scoring[4], while the other five top-order batsmen made a start without being able to build a big score. Darling, who was run out for 39, top-scored. Woodfull made 19, Richardson 32, Bradman 24 and McCabe 22.

Needing 160 to win, England achieved its goal with six wickets standing. Leyland made certain of the result with a hand of 86 and Paynter, 14 not out, fittingly lifted the score to four for 162 with a six off McCabe.

England had won back the Ashes, but Jardine persisted with bodyline in the fifth Test in Sydney. Australia, which dropped Ponsford for O'Brien, scored its highest total for the series due to some strong middle-order batting. After losing openers Richardson (0) and Woodfull (14), Bradman and O'Brien steadied the innings with 48 and 61 respectively. They were well supported by McCabe (73), Darling (85), Oldfield (52) and all-rounder Phillip Lee (42). Despite the ascendency of the Australian batsmen, Larwood picked up a useful four for 98 and then played an innings of 98 after being sent in as nightwatchman.

Larwood, who had nothing to lose in aiming to hit anything he fancied, made the difference between England trailing and leading on the first innings. Hammond scored 101 and the tourists' total of 454 gave them a lead of 19. Yet again Australia batted poorly in its second innings when it could manage only 182. Not once in the series did the home side reach 200 in its second knock and this time most of its runs came from Woodfull and Bradman who hit 67 and 71 respectively.

That left England needing 164 to win its fourth Test of the series, a target it passed with eight wickets standing. Even at that late stage of the series Jardine continued to become involved in controversy. This time the bitterness began when Jardine complained that fast bowler Alexander, making his one and only Test appearance, was running on to the pitch during his follow through. This riled both the bowler and the crowd, resulting in constant barracking from the spectators and some aggressive bowling by Alexander. One delivery struck Jardine a painful blow on the left hip and the crowd, unsportingly, roared its approval.

Neither Ponsford nor Woodfull played in Victoria's second match against the MCC in early March. Rigg led the home team which scored 327 and three for 177 in reply to the tourists' 321 and nine for 183 (dec.). At the time the game was considered a tie, but under today's rules it would be classed as a draw because Victoria's innings was incomplete.

The final game of the 1932–33 tour was against South Australia whose fast bowlers Tobin and Williams bowled to a field with five men on the leg-side. It was a weak imitation of bodyline by the South Australian captain Vic Richardson who was among the Australians in favour of retaliating to the England tactics. If Richardson had merely wished to thumb his nose at Jardine he made his point, but as far as worrying the opposing batsmen the South Australian bowlers didn't have the wherewithal to succeed.

So ended a singularly unhappy cricket tour in which the game was the loser. Jardine had certainly won back the Ashes and halved Bradman's yield of runs, but the harm done by bodyline went much further. Ponsford's effectiveness was reduced by more than half, Woodfull was unable to perform at his best and Kippax was forced from the Test arena. The bodyline tactics had a particularly unsettling effect on the players as indicated by the poor displays in each second innings. The series left both Ponsford and Woodfull with sour feelings for the game they loved. Each had been playing first-class cricket for a decade and, as men with young families, had reached the stage where retirement had to be given serious consideration.

It's a moot point whether the pair would have continued beyond the 1934 tour of England had the events of the 1932–33 series not transpired. Ponsford, especially, proved a tremendous run-getter in 1934. Each remained in the game after 1932–33 because he had a point to prove: that he wasn't going to be forced out of the game, to which he had contributed so much, by the supercilious attitude of an England captain. Nevertheless, the retirement of Ponsford and Woodfull in November 1934 was certainly influenced by bodyline. It seems that while Bradman was the primary target of bodyline, the two Victorians were also casualties.

Ironically Larwood, who had taken 33 wickets at 19.51 apiece in the 1932–33 Tests, also became a casualty of the series as the MCC used him as a scapegoat to restore Anglo-Australian relationships. Larwood continued to play with Nottinghamshire but did not play another Test and in 1950 migrated to Australia with his family.

Authorities in both Australia and England outlawed bodyline bowling. Controlling bodies in Australia were particularly concerned that it was being used in junior and country matches on concrete pitches. Fortunately for the game the problems were resolved quickly, but those involved at the highest level have never forgotten the unpleasantness of the summer of 1933.

Despite his abhorrence of bodyline bowling, Ponsford was able to look back on season 1932–33 with some satisfaction. Melbourne won the VCA premiership, beating St Kilda in the final, and 'Ponny' headed the association averages with 88.25. In the last home and away game he hit 85 in 135 minutes against Fitzroy, followed by 136 against St Kilda in the final. There were no semi-finals that season. In the final, St Kilda batted first and made 234 to which Melbourne replied with 356, Ponsford's score taking 261 minutes and including nine fours and two fives. Both the fives comprised a single and four overthrows. Lisle Nagel made the second highest score wth 62 while St Kilda's most successful bowler was Ted a'Beckett whose five for 72 included the wicket of Ponsford caught and bowled.

One of Ponsford's opponents in that game, St Kilda fast bowler Tom Leather, later became his brother-in-law when he married Bill's sister Dorothy. Leather, a former Caulfield Grammarian, appeared briefly with Victoria and was among the first Australian cricketers to tour India. That tour, in 1935–36, was financed by the Maharaja of Patiala and captained by Jack Ryder. Seven other Test representatives: Macartney, Ironmonger, Hendry, Oxenham, Love, Nagel and Alexander were also in the party. Leather eventually captured 63 wickets at 20.19 in his first-class career. He also played League football with North Melbourne and worked at the MCC with his brother-in-law.

NOTES

[1]The capacity of the ground was considerably less before the opening of the Southern Stand in 1937 and the Northern Stand in 1956.

[2]This was a record for the Adelaide Oval and an amazing one for a city with a population of little more than 300,000 at the time. Melbourne had more than three times that population from which to draw its huge crowds.

[3]There was an interesting but unpublicised sequel to the Oldfield incident. Jardine cabled Oldfield's wife, Ruth, that the England team wished her husband a speedy recovery and later he arranged through a Sydney friend for two dolls to be delivered to Oldfield's two young girls.

[4]Ponsford made only eight ducks in his entire first-class career, which represented 2.9 per cent of his 235 innings. Bradman made 16 ducks, which represented 4.7 per cent of his 338 innings.

SHIELD SUCCESS

THERE were no Test matches in season 1933–34 so attention focused on the Sheffield Shield competition and the likely candidates to be selected to tour England in 1934. At the time, an English tour was considered the ultimate reward for a first-class player as the financial gains were minimal. The return of Ponsford and Woodfull to the Victorian XI enabled the team to win back the Sheffield Shield, which it had last held in 1930–31. There were also two testimonial games to honour retired Test stars. In each game Woodfull hit a century.

In the wake of the bodyline series it was a quiet season although Woodfull must have thought otherwise when he was struck above the heart by a ball from Nash when Carlton met South Melbourne on the opening day of the Melbourne season. Woodfull continued to bat but was out in the same over, caught and bowled for 15. Meanwhile, at Northcote, Ponsford began the new season by sharing an unconquered double-century partnership with Keith Rigg. When Melbourne captain Hans Ebeling closed the innings at 5.05 pm the score was none for 238 with Ponsford 137 not out and Rigg 100 not out.[1] Northcote replied with 94 and four for 103.

Ponsford followed with 79 not out against the VCA Colts in the next game while Woodfull missed out on a hit as Carlton's scheduled match against Collingwood was cancelled owing to a ground dispute between Collingwood and the VCA.

Centuries to Ponsford and Rigg in Victoria's second innings against South Australia in Adelaide set up a convincing win at the start of the Shield season. Grimmett, who had taken seven for 80 in

Victoria's first innings, was on the receiving end in the second innings. Although he had top-scored with 52 in the first knock, Woodfull decided to open with Rigg and Ponsford when Victoria batted again. Rigg made 123 and 'Ponny' 122 in a stand of 240, which was 43 runs more than the entire side made in the first innings. Woodfull (22 not out) and Ben Barnett (65 not out) added 90 in an unfinished sixth-wicket partnership before the Victorian captain declared at five for 431.

South Australia, which had lost six wickets to 'Chuck' Fleetwood-Smith in making 228 in its first innings, lost another three wickets to him and six to Ironmonger in scoring 231 in its second innings. This left Victoria a 169-run winner.

A fortnight later a testimonial match was played at the MCG in honor of the veteran Victorian bowlers Ironmonger and Blackie. Richardson's XI batted first and was well-served by Fingleton (105), Rigg (94) and O'Brien (90) in making eight for 491 (dec.). In reply, Woodfull's XI reached nine for 350 before the innings was closed. Woodfull, who made 118, and Ponsford (42) gave the side a start of 104 and later McCabe contributed 82. At the end of the game Richardson's XI was four for 169, which included 101 from Bradman, in its second innings.

The second of the testimonials followed immediately in Sydney between New South Wales and The Rest. The game honored three New South Welshman of note: Herbie Collins, Charlie Kelleway and Tommy Andrews, and resulted in a narrow win to The Rest. McCabe's 110 was the outstanding innings in the New South Wales total of 273. The Rest answered with 255, Ponsford top-scoring with 70. Alan Kippax closed the New South Wales second innings at four for 390, having made an unbeaten 111 himself, to set The Rest the formidable task of scoring 409 for victory. Although Ponsford was out for nine, 'Woody' played a valuable hand of 129 while Len Darling (77) and 'Slinger' Nitschke (76) gave strong support. Nash (20 not out) and Hugh Chilvers (0 not out) were at the crease when The Rest reached its target with two wickets to spare. Kippax, who indulged himself in a rare bowling spell, took three for 10.

Victoria gained full points in Brisbane with an outright win against Queensland by an innings and 31 runs. Chasing a respectable tally of 349, Victoria lost Woodfull (16), O'Brien (8) and Ponsford (55) for 100 — all to Oxenham — before Rigg and Darling swung the game Victoria's way. The pair added 192 for the fourth wicket before Rigg was out for 92 and later Jack Scaife helped Darling put on 122 for the sixth wicket. Darling was out for 188, Scaife made 73 and Barnett proved that he could bat well and keep wickets by hitting 78. Oxenham sent down 53 overs in taking four for 111.

Queensland began its second innings disastrously, losing three wickets before scoring. Two of the wickets fell to paceman 'Bull' Alexander who took his third wicket to make the score four for 14. A hand of 97 by Eric Bensted enabled the northerners to avoid a rout, but the total of 162 was not enough to force Victoria to bat again. Ebeling finished with four for 42 and Alexander three for 25.

On that form one would have expected Victoria to add to its laurels when the two States played the return game at the MCG a fortnight later. Cricket, as we all know, can be unpredictable and such was the case when Queensland took first innings points in a drawn game. Victoria batted first and, despite half centuries from O'Brien and Darling, it managed only 204. Woodfull was out for 10 and Ponsford 23. Oxenham picked up the wickets of Ponsford, O'Brien, Bromley and Barnett for 36 runs.

For a time it seemed Victoria's modest score would be enough to lead Queensland which slumped to five for 90 and later eight for 153. But the tail wagged merrily, steadied by an unbeaten 33 from Oxenham, to lift the score to 242. Rigg, who had failed to score in the first innings at number four, opened the second innings with Ponsford and again made a duck. Darling made 33 and Bromley 57 while Ponsford patiently headed for a half century at the other end. When the match ended, 'Ponny' was 54 not out in a total of four for 155.

The traditional Christmas match against New South Wales at the MCG, in which Victoria took first innings points, was of little consequence for Ponsford and Woodfull although several players stood out. Bradman scored a fine double, making 187 not out and 77 not out, while O'Reilly's 12 wickets included nine for 50 in Victoria's second innings. The tall New South Welshman bowled four of his victims. The one wicket he missed was that of Barnett who was bowled by paceman, Alan McGilvray. Fleetwood-Smith also had a good match, taking seven for 138 in New South Wales' first innings.

Woodfull (60), O'Brien (86) and Darling (91) helped Victoria to a solid 382 in its first innings, which proved slightly out of New South Wales' reach despite Bradman's form. Leading by 27 runs, Victoria seemed set to consolidate when it reached three for 144 in its second innings, but O'Reilly had other ideas and the home side slumped to be all out for 200. Darling top-scored with 53 and Ponsford made 40. When time ran out, New South Wales was well on the way to victory at one for 144.

Ponsford driving a car instead of a ball.

Ponsford hits the ball past the gully fieldsman during his highest Test innings of 266, at The Oval in 1934.

A sporting incident that incensed a nation. Bill Woodfull staggers away from the wicket after being struck above the heart by a delivery from Harold Larwood. Woodfull's widow attributes his death in 1965 to that injury.

Woodfull ducks a Larwood delivery in the Brisbane Test, 1933 as the packed leg-side field awaits the ball. The bodyline fieldsmen (left to right) are Leyland, Allen, Ames, Jardine, Verity and Sutcliffe.

During the Victorian first innings, when he made 30, Ponsford passed Warwick Armstrong's Victorian record of 6732 runs. 'Ponny', who finished the season and his career with 6902 runs, remained the record-holder until Bill Lawry exceeded the total in 1970–71.[2]

In Woodfull's absence, Ponsford captained Victoria against South Australia at the MCG and celebrated the arrival of 1934 with a five-wicket win. The visitors batted first and, thanks to a hand of 115 from Albert Lonergan, reached 313 amid a fine piece of bowling by Fleetwood-Smith. His return of eight for 111 included six batsmen who were bowled. Victoria replied with 366 which was due to Ponsford's 94 and a career best of 161 from Ernie Bromley. There was an unusual dismissal when Bromley played a ball from A. J. Ryan which the bowler deflected onto the stumps with non-striker Ebeling out of his crease. Ebeling had made 17.

Lonergan made his second century of the match, an even 100, in South Australia's second innings which yielded a modest 198. Fleetwood-Smith added four for 47 to his earlier success. Needing 146 for victory, the home State was given a start of 53 by Ponsford and Rigg before 'Ponny', for only the second time in a first-class match, was out hit wicket. He had made 27. Rigg went on to make 50 before being caught off Grimmett who captured four for 52 in Victoria's final score of five for 146.

That game was destined to be Ponsford's last with Victoria. He did not make the trip to Sydney for the return game against New South Wales and, with Woodfull, had retired before the 1934–35 Shield season began. Woodfull scored 83 and 11 in his final game with Victoria, a drawn match in which New South Wales earned first innings points after hitting eight for 672 (dec.). Bill Brown, a young opener of great promise, hit 205 while Fingleton (145) and Bradman (128) also made centuries. In reply, Victoria was far from disgraced in making 407. Jack Scaife, a Fitzroy batsman, top-scored with 120 and Bromley made 92. Forced to follow on, Victoria was in trouble when Woodfull and O'Brien were out with only 22 scored, but re-covered to finish with five for 274. The recovery was due chiefly to Darling (93) and Scaife whose 80 complemented his first innings century.

Scaife's form in Sydney also enabled him to lead the Victorian averages with 58.40 from Ponsford on 55.75 and Darling 54.90.

Ponsford and Woodfull were naturally chosen to tour England in 1934, a series that was vital to the future of Test cricket after the rupture caused by bodyline in the 1932–33 series. Five Victorians — Barnett, Bromley, Darling, Ebeling and Fleetwood-Smith, and New

South Wales Bill Brown and Arthur Chipperfield made their first tour.

The customary pre-tour games were played in Hobart, Launceston and Perth to sharpen the players' form and Woodfull, in particular, was in pleasing touch. In Launceston, where Ponsford didn't play, Woodfull hit 126 and his opening partner, Brown, made 96. In Hobart the same pair again made 222 between them. This time Woodfull scored 124 — in only 150 minutes — and Brown 98. In Perth the Australian XI was five for 274, chasing Western Australia's 305, before rain washed out play early on the third day.

Meanwhile, Woodfull had headed the VCA averages for the fourth time with 158.50 from the four innings he played with Carlton during the 1933–34 season. Ponsford, dismissed only once in making 233 runs, had a higher average but had less than the minimum 250 runs needed to qualify for the honor.

NOTES

[1]Rigg, who eventually played eight Tests and made 5544 runs in first-class games with 14 centuries, was highly regarded by Ponsford. 'Riggy was a fine batsman, but should have gone a lot further than he did,' recalled Ponsford in 1986.

[2]Victoria's 10 leading run-scorers with their average in brackets are: W. Lawry 7618 (51.47), W. Ponsford 6902 (86.27), L. Hassett 6825 (63.19), G. Yallop 6815 (47.99), W. Armstrong 6732 (52.18), I. Redpath 6103 (41.51), J. Ryder 5674 (45.75), W. Woodfull 5484 (75.12), J. Potter 5101 (42.50), N. Harvey 4914 (50.14).

A WINNING
FAREWELL

ILL Woodfull won back the Ashes in 1934, the second time he had achieved that distinction in England. It wasn't until 1953 that they again changed hands. Both Woodfull and Ponsford enjoyed much success on their third and final tour of England. At times Ponsford reached the great heights he attained in the mid-1920s. Woodfull intimated before the end of the tour that he would no longer appear with Australia and Victoria. Ponsford took a little longer to make up his mind, but he also felt it was time to step down.

By 1934 the economic depression had eased although evidence of the struggle for employment was still apparent in the working-class suburbs of the capital cities. In Perth the first pavlova was cooked by Bert Sasche and the ABC also made a contribution to Australian culture by synthetically broadcasting the Tests in England. With the aid of the latest cabled scores and clever sound effects, Australians were able to learn the latest cricket news with a dash of entertainment before retiring to bed, rather than waiting for the morning newspaper or radio breakfast news.

While radio had made big advances in the previous decade, the cinema was being revolutionised. Just as cricket had won a mass audience through its star attractions such as Ponsford, Woodfull, Bradman and McCabe, the film industry was booming thanks to Spencer Tracy, Katherine Hepburn, Claudette Colbert, Clark Gable and others.

It was with this background that the Australian cricketers sailed for England on a tour that, for those involved in the game, hoped would heal the rift caused by the unfortunate events of the 1932–33 summer.

Australia could hardly have made a better start to the 1934 tour than it did against Worcestershire. In winning by an innings and 297 runs the tourists showed that Bradman, who hit 206, would again be a prolific scorer and spinners O'Reilly and Grimmett were heading for a good season. Woodfull began the tour with a hand of 48 and Ponsford hit 13.

Ponsford was again dismissed cheaply in the tourists' next match, against Leicestershire, but the third game found the Victorian opener at his brilliant best. Playing Cambridge University, the Australians scored four for 418 on the opening day and declared at five for 481 early the next day. Ponsford made 229 not out in a very confident innings lasting 370 minutes and including 19 fours. Apart from a 'hot' caught and bowled chance at 140, his display was without fault and might have produced even more runs had many fine drives not been fielded so well.

Brown, who hit 105, helped Ponsford add 262 for the fifth wicket and Darling also was prominent with 98. Cambridge replied by making 158 and 160, Grimmett capturing nine for 74 in the first innings.

Memories of Ponsford's relentless scoring for Victoria in 1926–27 and 1927–28 were revived in the next game, against the MCC at Lord's, when he made another unbeaten double century. This time he was 281 not out when Woodfull closed the innings at six for 559, having been associated with McCabe in a then world record stand of 389 for the third wicket.[1]

The MCC had batted first and compiled a strong 362 after Test batsmen Hendren and Wyatt had hit 135 and 72 respectively, despite some good bowling by Wall (six for 74). The tourists lost Woodfull for 20 and Bradman for five, but Ponsford played one of the finest innings of his illustrious career and McCabe ran into top form with 192 in 265 minutes. Ponsford batted for 420 minutes and hit 26 fours. His partnership with McCabe beat the previous world third-wicket record of 375 which belonged to Hendren and J. W. Hearne who were playing for Middlesex against Hampshire at Southampton in 1923. It was rather ironic that Hendren was in the field when the new record was created. The MCC narrowly averted an innings defeat, being eight for 182 at the end of the game with Wyatt 102 not out.

At Chelmsford against Essex, after making 510 runs in two innings without being dismissed, Ponsford was out without scoring. Woodfull made 55, but the plaudits went to Chipperfield who hit 175 and soon after made an unbeaten century against Hampshire. His 116 not out in the latter game was most timely, as Hampshire had made 420 and then removed Woodfull for two, Bradman for nought and Brown for a duck due to a great spell of bowling by paceman Baring. The Australians recovered from three for 10 through the efforts of McCabe (79), Darling (96) and Chipperfield to reach 433.

Against Middlesex, Woodfull and Ponsford were both lbw to Smith — a fast bowler from Wiltshire — for nought before Bradman steadied the side with 160. This enabled the Australians to reach 345 and go on to a 10-wicket win.

Big scoring by both sides ruled out a result against Surrey at The Oval. The county batted first and declared at seven for 475 after veteran Andy Sandham had made 219. Ponsford and McCabe opened the Australians' innings and weren't parted until they had scored 239. The Victorian was out for 125 in an attractive and versatile display which included 17 fours. McCabe batted for another three hours, making 240 in a knock that included 29 fours. Bradman also got among the runs with 77 and the tourists finished with a massive 629. When the game finished Surrey was two for 162 in its second innings.

Woodfull was one of the three Australians to score a century against Lancashire. McCabe hit 142 in the first innings, which reached 367, and Woodfull (172 not out) and Brown (119) dominated the second innings total of three for 338. Woodfull batted 290 minutes and hit 12 fours, sharing a second-wicket partnership of 281 with Brown. It was tremendous form on the eve of the first Test.

At that stage of the tour Ponsford headed the averages from McCabe, Chipperfield, Barnett and Bradman. Brown and Chipperfield were chosen to make their Test debut at Trent Bridge, Nottingham. Both succeeded and helped Australia to a one-nil lead in the series.

After winning the toss, Woodfull and Ponsford gave Australia a useful start of 77. Ponsford was the first out, caught at the wicket off fast bowler Ken Farnes for 53, and Woodfull followed at 88 when he was caught in the gully by Verity for 26. Farnes was again the bowler. Brown (22) and Bradman (29) made a start without getting going and Verity bowled Darling for only four. At five for 153 Australia's sound start had not been consolidated, but McCabe and Chipperfield then took the score to 207 before rain stopped play.

The following day McCabe was out to Farnes for 65 and Chipperfield, 99 not out at lunch, was caught at the wicket off Farnes from the second ball after the break without adding to his score. His consolation was that he had helped Australia recover to a sound position and an eventual first innings total of 374. Farnes took the bowling honors for England with five for 102.

England, four for 128 at stumps, might well have failed to compile 200 the next day, but for a seventh-wicket stand worth 101 between Hendren (79) and Geary (53), which enabled the team to reach 268. The bulk of the bowling was done by Grimmett and O'Reilly who returned five for 81 and four for 75 respectively.

Australia lost Woodfull for two and Ponsford for a patient five early in its second innings, but a fourth-wicket partnership of 112 between Brown and McCabe lifted it into a strong position. McCabe's 88 and Brown's 73 were by far the best examples of batsmanship before Woodfull closed the innings at eight for 273. This left England 380 to win in 285 minutes, a target beyond the batsmen. Woodfull's declaration left just enough time for Grimmett and O'Reilly to spin them out for 141.

The match finished at 6.20 pm, 10 minutes before stumps, on the final day and Woodfull came in for criticism for leaving his declaration so late. At five for 134 it seemed the home team would avert defeat, but the last five wickets crashed for seven runs and the Australian captain's tactics paid off. Certainly he cut it fine, but with Grimmett and O'Reilly delivering an over in next to no time there were constant opportunities to wind up the innings. Grimmett sent down 47 overs in taking three for 39 and O'Reilly bowled 41.4 overs to snare seven for 54.

The tourists played another tight finish in their next game, against Northamptonshire, only this time they were left one wicket short of victory. The county was in no position to win, needing a further 199 runs, but the one wicket standing allowed them to escape with a draw. The Australians beat the Gentlemen of England by eight wickets in the only other game before the second Test at Lord's.

Australia was forced to make one change because Ponsford had influenza. Bromley came into the side as a middle-order batsman with Brown being promoted from number three to the opening position. The match belonged to left-arm spinner Hedley Verity whose total of 15 wickets gave England victory by an innings and 38 runs.

England batted first and the game was very much in the balance at five for 182 after Chipperfield had proved a surprise packet with the ball, taking the choice wickets of Sutcliffe, Hammond and Wyatt. Centuries to Leyland (109) and Ames (120) lifted England to a total of 440. In reply Australia seemed set to challenge England's supremacy when it reached two for 203 due largely to 105 from Brown. Then came a slump with three wickets falling for two runs and the side never recovered. A rain-affected pitch did not help matters.

Trailing by 156 runs, Australia followed on and, despite losing Brown for two and Bradman for 13, the resolute defence of Woodfull helped push the score to three for 94. Verity then became unplayable and five wickets tumbled for only one run. Woodfull top-scored with 43 in 105 minutes in his team's total of 118, while Verity followed his first innings haul of seven for 61 with eight for 43.

Woodfull again made the highest score, being run out for 84, when the tourists visited Taunton to play Somerset. The county was dismissed for 116 in both its innings, O'Reilly picking up nine for 38 in the first innings. The second game against Surrey also resulted in a win for the Australians, this time by six wickets, which preceded the third Test at Old Trafford, Manchester.

In a match where the bat generally dominated the ball, England set the scene when it scored nine for 627 (dec.) after suffering a brief setback on the first day when O'Reilly dismissed opener Cyril Walters, then Wyatt and Hammond in four balls. Walters had scored 52, Wyatt was bowled first ball, Hammond glanced a four and was then bowled. Hendren (132) and Leyland (153) took the initiative and their success was followed by half centuries from lower order batsmen Ames, Allen and Verity. Meanwhile, O'Reilly continued to toil away and from 59 overs earned seven for 189.

Ponsford and Brown began Australia's long chase, but at 34 the Victorian was out for 12. Brown, justifying the faith Woodfull had in him as an opener, added 196 with McCabe for the second wicket. He contributed 72 and McCabe 137. Woodfull followed with 73 before being run out, but the chances of avoiding the follow-on diminished as the rest of the batsmen failed to settle after making a useful start. O'Reilly and Wall rescued the side with an invaluable 37 for the tenth wicket, leaving Australia 136 runs behind. The total of 491 exceeded by 14 the follow-on point.

Sutcliffe and Walters followed their first innings half-centuries with 69 not out and 50 not out before Wyatt declared England's second innings at none for 123. Australia lost Brown for nought with only one run scored in its second innings, but Ponsford (30 not out) and McCabe (33 not out) steered the side to one for 66 in the time remaining. Clearly the match was inconclusive although England was entitled to say it had the better of the draw.

Between the third and fourth Tests, the tourists beat Derbyshire by nine wickets and drew with Yorkshire at Sheffield. Bradman, whose five Test innings had yielded only 133 runs, ran into good form in the latter game with 140.

Cricket devotees had often wondered what would have happened had Ponsford and Bradman struck their best form while batting together. In 1931 the pair had put on 223 for the second wicket against the West Indies in Brisbane, but everyone knew that the potential was there for a huge stand if the two champions recaptured the application which earned them quadruple centuries. Finally at Headingley, Leeds, in July 1934 they did so.

After dismissing England for 200, Australia was in trouble at stumps on the first day, having lost Brown for 15 and both Oldfield and Woodfull without scoring. All three wickets had fallen to Bowes. On the second day Ponsford, who was 22, resumed with Bradman who was yet to face a ball. The pair lifted the score from a sorry three for 39 to a healthy four for 427. England's bowlers toiled away as the two champions batted through the pre-lunch session, were still unparted at tea with the score three for 329, and midway through the third session of the day seemed likely to finish the day unconquered.

Ponsford, who had given three difficult chances on his way to 181, was less fortunate with the total at 427. As he played a pull shot off Verity to the boundary his left leg swung back slightly and dislodged a bail. What a way to end such a grand partnership! Ponsford, who had batted for 375 minutes and hit 21 fours during his long stay, had helped add 388 for the fourth wicket.

At stumps Bradman was still batting, having hit 39 fours and two sixes in a score of 271 not out. McCabe was 18 not out. The total of four for 494 was hardly an encouragement for the bowlers on the third day. Yet it was the bowling that drew the plaudits when the game resumed. McCabe's fifth-wicket stand with Bradman, which was worth 90, ended at 517 when he was bowled by Bowes for 27. Bradman completed his second triple century and soon after was bowled by Bowes for 304[2]. Bowes, who also bowled Darling, bowled five batsmen in taking a splendid six for 142 off 50 overs. Bradman and Ponsford scored all but 99 of Australia's total of 584. England was six for 229 in its second innings when rain saved it from almost certain defeat.

Following his massive stand with Bradman, Ponsford was associated in a first-wicket partnership worth 183 with Woodfull against Gloucestershire. Ponsford was not at his best in batting for more than three hours for 54, but Woodfull hit out where possible and his innings of 131 included a six.

Woodfull was in even better form at Swansea, batting all day in making an unbeaten 228 in a score of seven for 440 (dec.). His dashing six-hour display included 20 fours and he received strong support from Kippax who made 77. Players wore black armbands as a mark of respect to Ponsford's father Bill, who had died just before the match started.

Neither Ponsford nor Woodfull played against Warwickshire and in the match before the fifth Test, against Nottinghamshire, memories of the 1932–33 series were revived when Voce bowled leg-theory in the first innings. Voce modified his tactics by not bowling bumpers, but his return of eight for 66 restricted the Australians to 237. Larwood did not play, ostensibly because of injury, and Bradman was rested.

The county was all out for 183 and when they batted a second time the tourists compiled two for 230 (dec.) after losing Woodfull for only one. Brown scored 100 not out and Kippax an unbeaten 75. Voce bowled only two overs in this innings due, officially, to shin soreness, but unofficially the Australian management had complained to the Nottinghamshire committee regarding Voce's tactics. When the tourists entered the field for Nottinghamshire's second innings they were hooted by spectators. The country managed to avert defeat, being six for 128 when the game finished.

The fifth Test, at The Oval, resulted in an overwhelming win to Australia and Woodfull had the satisfaction of winning back the Ashes on his thirty-seventh birthday. The basis for the win was a phenomenal second-wicket partnership of 451 between Ponsford and Bradman. In less than a day both players made a double century to put Australia in an unbeatable position.

Ponsford and Brown had opened the innings, but with only 21 on the board Brown was out for 10. Bradman joined 'Ponny' and the pair again hammered the bowling unmercifully, as they had at Headingley. Once more Bradman scored more quickly than his partner, but the difference was not all that great. Ponsford was one batsman who could bat in tandem with 'The Don'.

The huge partnership was broken shortly before stumps when Bradman edged a delivery from Bowes to Ames. In 310 minutes he had batted faultlessly for 244, which included 32 fours and one six. By stumps Ponsford was 205 in a total of two for 475 and when play resumed McCabe was out cheaply at 488. This brought Woodfull and Ponsford together for the last time in a Test and they appeared set to add another century stand to their long list of partnerships. They had put on 86 and Ponsford had raised his score to 266 when 'Ponny', trying to avoid a rising ball from Allen, trod on his wicket.

Ponsford had played his highest Test innings although technically it wasn't his best. He had given several difficult chances before he reached 116, but during his 455 minutes at the crease he showed the concentration and application that made him such a great player. It was a plucky rather than brilliant innings, his seventh Test century and one that included 28 fours and one five.

Woodfull made 49 in 145 minutes before being bowled by Bowes. Although it was the third highest score of the innings, it was not Woodfull at his best. From five for 626 the innings fell away, despite 42 not out from Oldfield, to finish at 701. Bowes and Allen each took four wickets, conceding 164 and 170 runs respectively.

England began its long chase with an opening stand of 104 by Walters, who hit 64, and Sutcliffe. But the bright start soon gave way to a collapse. Five wickets fell for 38 before Leyland restored order by making 110 and Ames helped out with a useful 33 until he was forced to retire hurt. Despite its total of 321, England was not asked to follow on.

A third-wicket partnership of 150 between Bradman (77) and McCabe (70) highlighted Australia's second innings of 327. Ponsford's final Test innings yielded 22 runs and Woodfull's brought 13. This left England the impossible task of scoring 608 to win with only 10 batsmen (Ames couldn't take part) although a draw would have enabled England to retain the Ashes.

McCabe scored a vital break when he opened the bowling with Ebeling and dismissed Walters and veteran Frank Woolley with only three runs scored. As useful as McCabe the bowler had proved, Woodfull gave him only five overs and called in Grimmett and O'Reilly. For a time Sutcliffe and Hammond showed fine resistance to the Australian spin duo, but when O'Reilly caught and bowled Hammond for 43 the innings declined. Grimmett helped himself to five wickets, restricting England's total to 145 and leaving Australia the winner of the Test by 562 runs.

O'Reilly and Grimmett took 53 of the 71 wickets captured by Australia's bowlers in the series and in both cases did not pay a big price. O'Reilly's 28 wickets cost him 24.93 each and Grimmett paid 26.72 runs for each of his 25 wickets. Ponsford won the batting average in a photo-finish from Bradman, finishing with 94.83 to 94.75. Woodfull dropped to 28.50, but his value to the side was still high.

Four more first-class games were played after the fifth Test. Ponsford rounded off a most successful tour with 82 not out against Kent at Canterbury and 92 against Leveson-Gower's XI at Scarborough, while Woodfull made an unbeaten 62 against an England XI at Folkestone.

Woodfull had signified his intention to retire from first-class cricket while Ponsford was thinking about his future but had not come to a decision. The VCA, aware of the enormous contribution both players had made to interstate and international cricket, decided to arrange a testimonial match at the MCG in November soon after the players arrived home.

The game was between Woodfull's XI, a Test side with the exception of Bradman who didn't play, and Richardson's XI which comprised several players with Test experience and others destined to make the grade.

Richardson's XI batted first and made a modest 196, leaving the way clear for Ponsford and Woodfull to bat the following afternoon, a Saturday, before the largest crowd. Brown and McCabe opened late on the first day and were parted after a rain-interrupted start on the Saturday when McCabe tried to turn a ball from paceman Ernie McCormick. The ball struck him on the right hand, breaking a small bone. Brown and Chipperfield were both out cheaply and at two for 25 Ponsford came to the crease amid a great reception from the crowd.

Woodfull joined him at three for 57 after Kippax was out. The Australian captain was cheered all the way to the wicket and the band played *For He's a Jolly Good Fellow*. He scored a single to leg and then lunch was taken. After the break the sun shone and the famous batting partnership flourished. In only 86 minutes the pair had added 100 and another 32 runs were put on before Ponsford was out in unusual circumstances. Ponsford stepped down the pitch to C. J. Hill, a New South Wales bowler, and snicked the ball past the wicket where it rebounded from Barnett's pads on to the stumps. Ponsford was run out, having made 83 in 148 minutes.

At tea Woodfull was 67 and light rain returned. When play resumed the retiring Australian leader pressed on to his 49th first-class century, a chanceless knock which took 172 minutes. He then began to hit out and at 111 was caught by McCormick at long-on off the bowling of Nagel.

The crowd had built up to 22,637 and when Woodfull returned to the dressing room, Ponsford, looking across to the area that now holds the Southern stand, said to Woodfull: 'Don't close the game just yet, there's another fellow coming in.'

Soon after, Woodfull's XI was all out for 316. With a lead of 120 but eager to see the game survive for four days, Woodfull said to Grimmett on the third day: 'No leg breaks, no appeals, there has to be a fourth day.'[3] He also brought on Darling, believing he would not dislodge opener Jack Fingleton. A delivery from Darling, about a metre outside the leg stump, was glanced by Fingleton and magnificently caught by Oldfield down the leg side. Not a word was spoken and the ball was returned to the bowler.

Fingleton was out cheaply but Vic Richardson went on to make a century in his team's total of 399 and a fourth day's play was ensured. Woodfull's XI needed 280 to win and 4783 people were at the MCG to see the side achieve the target with seven wickets to spare. O'Reilly, sent in as a nightwatchman late on the third day, helped Brown put on 54 for the first wicket before being caught at the wicket for 19. Ponsford joined Brown and the pair added 103 in the next hour and a half. Ponsford was out for 48, caught in slips off McCormick, trying to cut a ball on a good length. At 189 Brown was out for 102, but Kippax and Darling added the 91 runs still required.

As the match ended so, too, did the illustrious first-class careers of Bill Ponsford and Bill Woodfull. Both continued to play District cricket, Woodfull for two more seasons and Ponsford for another four, but effectively their days as great players were finished. Fortunately for Australia there were other fine young opening batsmen to replace them, namely Bill Brown and Jack Fingleton, and when Don Bradman became captain in 1936 he proved a worthy successor in that area.

Ponsford and Woodfull shared £2084 ($4168) as a result of the testimonial game. At the time £1000 had considerable purchasing power and was more than many workmen earned in a year, although it can also be argued that for two who rated so highly in their field it wasn't as big a send-off as they deserved.

One final accolade, which Woodfull had enjoyed in 1927, was Ponsford's choice as one of *Wisden's* five cricketers of the year in 1935. Two other Australian players of note, Stan McCabe and Bill O'Reilly, were also included that year.

Woodfull ranks among the greatest of Australian captains, being greatly admired for his leadership qualities and the fine example he set as a batsman. Noted Australian cricket writer Ray Robinson, who won much praise for his study of Australian captains in his book *On Top Down Under*, said of Woodfull: 'The kernel of Woodfull's captaincy was the way he got so much from each man. Their esteem was their response to his personal qualities of common-sense, straightforwardness, tolerance, consideration and unselfish service to his side. Bill was so truthful he could not utter even an off-white lie. More than any predecessor, he showed interest in their personal welfare, as well as their field performances — all about their families, problems and hopes. I know of no other national captain who held players' trust and loyalty to such a degree, though cricketers who played for Sir Frank Worrell and Richie Benaud would scarcely think they could be outdone. In a game of delicate balance between individual aims and team needs, Woodfull's unrivalled selflessness won fidelity bordering on devotion.'

NOTES

[1]Ponsford's 281 not out remains the highest score by an Australian at Lord's. Only five other Australians have made a double century at Lord's. They are Warwick Armstrong, 248 not out versus Gentlemen of England 1905; Don Bradman, 254 versus England 1930 and 278 versus MCC 1938; Bill Brown, 206 not out versus England 1938; Neil Harvey, 225 versus MCC 1956; and Lindsay Hassett, 200 not out versus Gentlemen of England 1948.

[2]Bradman's innings had taken 420 minutes and included 43 fours and two sixes.

[3]Woodfull recounted this incident at his farewell dinner at Melbourne High School in 1962.

LIFE MOVES ON

BILL Woodfull was 37 and Bill Ponsford 34 on retirement. Ever since that decision cricket followers have argued that 'Ponny' left big cricket too early. The argument is based on the assumption that because he had such a successful tour of England in 1934 Ponsford would have maintained that form for at least another few years. No doubt he would have, being such a great player, but the decision was his and he had sound reasons. For more than a decade he had been playing first-class cricket and had achieved an incredible amount of success. In those days the biggest reward for a player, apart from a testimonial which was confined to champions, was to tour England. Ponsford had earned three tours of England and, as a man with a young family, he felt obliged to spend more time at home. In addition, the nastiness of the bodyline series had diminished Ponsford's enthusiasm for the game.

In later years a number of other champions retired at a similar age to Ponsford. Arthur Morris and Richie Benaud were both 33, Neil Harvey was 34 and Bill Lawry 35. Bob Simpson was only 32 when he initially retired although he did make an unexpected comeback a decade later.

Woodfull, also a veteran of more than a dozen years in first-class cricket, had made three tours of England and captained Australia in 25 consecutive Tests. He, too, had the responsibility of a growing family and was very keen to make the most of his career in education. Even before his cricket days had finished, Woodfull the school master, did not mix the game with his teaching at Melbourne High, much to the chagrin of students who automatically expected him to be the cricket coach. Nor did he make a big thing about his own knowledge of the game and achievements. Fellow teachers in later years found him reticent about cricket.

Meanwhile, Ponsford's loss to the Australian and Victorian teams was a decided gain for Melbourne. In four seasons he scored more than 2000 runs and helped the club win the VCA premiership each year. Although he didn't win the batting average he twice topped the aggregate with 829 runs in 1935-36 and 744 runs in 1937-38. His ability to take part in a huge partnership remained and with Keith Rigg he shared an undefeated opening stand of 331 against University in 1935-36. Ponsford was 165 not out and Rigg 158 not out.

Despite Ponsford's presence, Melbourne did not depend on him for its success. It could lose him cheaply and still make a winning score as it did in the 1934-35 final against Collingwood when 'Ponny' was out for one and Rigg and Len Darling each made a century. The following year Ponsford was out for two and Melbourne trailed Fitzroy by 72 runs on the first innings. Fitzroy struggled in its second innings, leaving Melbourne 162 to win. This time Ponsford top-scored with 43 and Melbourne acquired the runs with five wickets in hand.

In 1936-37 Melbourne beat Richmond in the final, Ponsford contributing 100 of his team's 248 in reply to Richmond's 194. The Richmond attack included Test fast bowler Ernie McCormick who took five for 63 off 16 overs. There were no semi-finals in 1937-38 and Melbourne, which comfortably headed the ladder, played off for the premiership with second team Fitzroy. Melbourne eventually made it four flags in a row, but for much of the game Fitzroy seemed likely to win.

Melbourne batted first and was dismissed for 117. Rigg top-scored with 35 and Ponsford made nine. Fitzroy replied with 228, of which Jack Frederick — better known as a slow bowler — hit 60 and Maurie Sievers, who had played three Tests, was run out for 49. The Nagel twins took four wickets each for Melbourne. In its second innings Melbourne improved to score 239, Ponsford providing 36 and Vern Nagel 42. This left Fitzroy needing 129 runs to win. Lisle Nagel swung the game Melbourne's way by taking six for 48 in a total of 115. Melbourne had won by 13 runs.

The match marked the end of Ponsford's 22-year association with club cricket in Melbourne. A keen fisherman, he later took up lawn bowls and played pennant with MCC.

The retirement of Ponsford and Woodfull meant that the Australian team touring England in 1938 was without some familiar faces to English players and crowds, although Woodfull attended as a press correspondent. Woodfull also took his family and lived in the London suburb of Wimbledon. His sons Jack and Bill attended school, while daughter Jill was still a baby.

On returning home, Bill Woodfull continued to teach at Melbourne high School until the end of 1940. He spent the next two years at Bendigo High School and it was while in Bendigo that he sought to enlist for war service. Rejected on medical grounds due to his boyhood attack of rheumatic fever, Woodfull instead taught navigation to the Royal Australian Air Force (RAAF). While his family was pleased that he didn't go into the forces, his son Bill recalled that 'Dad was a bit upset that he was rejected'.

At the start of the 1943 school year, Bill Woodfull took up the first of his three postings as a school principal. The Upwey Higher Elementary School in the Dandenong Ranges, east of Melbourne, was a relatively new addition to the Education Department (having been opened in 1937) but it grew, and during Mr Woodfull's time as headmaster was upgraded to a high school. The Woodfulls made their home at nearby Belgrave.

As the years rolled by Woodfull occasionally reflected on cricket with his family and certain names shone strongly despite the passage of time. One was Jack Hobbs who had approached Woodfull early in the third Test in 1926 after Bardsley had been dismissed first ball and Macartney was on his way to the crease. Hobbs could have ignored Woodfull, but instead he gave the nervous Australian opener a few consoling words as the field awaited the incoming batsman. Macartney dashed to a century before lunch and later in the day Woodfull completed his first Test hundred. Hobbs' friendliness was never forgotten.

Of the English bowlers, Woodfull, like Ponsford, had great admiration for Tate. He naturally considered Grimmett and O'Reilly the greatest Australian bowlers of his time, but felt 'Chuck' Fleetwood-Smith was a risk to use in a Test. He described team mate Ponsford as one of the greatest cricketers Australia has had and 'definitely the greatest batsman I saw against slow bowlers'.

'Dad never spoke too much about Larwood,' Bill Woodfull junior recalled. 'If he didn't have anything nice to say, he would say nothing.'

Therefore the name Jardine wasn't mentioned?

'Not a lot,' replied Bill junior.

During the 1940s Woodfull, who believed Ponsford retired too soon, looked at the spin bowlers of the day and said to his sons: ' 'Ponny'

Bill Woodfull chats to King George V during a visit to Windsor Castle in 1934. The king, who was very interested in cricket and attended games, had much admiration for Woodfull. Pictured (left to right) are Alan Kippax, Bill Ponsford, Bill O'Reilly, Bill Woodfull, King George V, Arthur Chipperfield, Queen Mary and Hans Ebeling.

One of the schools at which Bill Woodfull was principal — Melbourne High.

Both men played many long innings during their cricketing days and both have lived a long life. Sir Donald Bradman (left) and Bill Ponsford revive old days at the Sport Australia Hall of Fame opening in 1985. At the time they were aged 77 and 85, respectively.

would never have let these fellows hit the pitch. He would have murdered them.'

In 1948 Bill Woodfull returned to Melbourne High School, this time as vice-principal. Six years later he began a two-year term as headmaster of Box Hill High School, which, like Melbourne, was one of the few boys' high schools in Victoria. By coincidence Woodfull went to Box Hill at the same time as Ian Huntington who joined the school from university to take charge of the physical education department. Huntington, a left-hand batsman who made five first-class centuries, represented Victoria 46 times from 1953–54 to 1963–64 and hit 2233 runs at an average of 34.35 an innings. While at Box Hill High School, Woodfull introduced inter-house choral singing which reflected his interest in music, especially Gilbert and Sullivan. Ponsford, by contrast, did not have any musical interest to speak of.

The appointment of Bill Woodfull as principal of Melbourne High School culminated his rise to the top of the teaching profession. He held this post from 1956 until his retirement on August 23 1962. As a pupil, master, vice-principal and principal he had spent almost 30 years at Melbourne High School. His predecessors as principal, Sir Alan Ramsay and Brigadier George Langley were also old boys of the school.

Woodfull was guest of honor at the Melbourne High School Old Boys Association annual dinner to mark his retirement. Four other former Australian cricket captains attended: Vic Richardson, who came over from Adelaide, Jack Ryder, Lindsay Hassett and Ian Johnson. Ponsford attended, as did the patriarch of Australian cricket followers, Prime Minister Robert Menzies. Other players of note at the dinner were Bert Oldfield, Bert Ironmonger, Jack Ellis and Ernie McCormick.

Menzies, at his eloquent best, told of the occasion he addressed a gathering in a Goulburn Valley town at the time an England-Australia Test was about to start. His host, also a cricket lover, had arranged to have a law clerk listen to the cricket broadcast in the ante-room at the local hall where Menzies was speaking. The speech had hardly got underway when the fire bell rang and the hall emptied. 'Will they come back?' Menzies asked the chairman. 'Oh, yes. I've arranged to have the cricket scores.'

The people returned and the speech resumed. Then came the first report of the cricket. Australia batting — Woodfull 15 not out, Ponsford five not out. 'Woodfull must have received a couple of no balls,' Menzies told the Old Boys' dinner. The next report gave Woodfull 25 not out and Ponsford 27 not out.

'We got to a stage where this Bill was leading that Bill by one and the strain got too great. We declared the meeting closed, someone moved a vote of confidence in me and I retired to the host's home to listen to the cricket,' Menzies recalled.

On a more serious note the Prime Minister said of Woodfull: 'Most people in the course of their lives manage to make some enemies, manage to have some knowledgeable critics, become involved in incidents. No captain of Australia ever went out of the game leaving behind him a more untouched reputation, a greater affection and a greater respect than William Maldon Woodfull.'

'This old friend of mine will retire and sit under his own vine and fig tree while I'm still being chased up and down the entire country. It isn't right. Prime Ministers should compulsorily retire at 65 with provision for double pay if their retirement has to be backdated from 67 to 65. You are being honored because of your character, your immense skill, your great wisdom and above all your warm, simple humanity.'

Woodfull, sticking to his resolve that his profession transcended his sporting achievements, said: 'It has been a great honour to captain Australia on the field, a much greater honour to captain Melbourne High School.'

In keeping with Bill Woodfull as an achiever, his brothers also proved capable men in their various endeavors. Balfour became head of the Melbourne City Council electric supply, Melville was general manager of the Australian Government Aircraft Factory at Fishermen's Bend and Colin was director of the Royal Agricultural Society for 20 years until his retirement.

Both Bill Woodfull's sons became dentists and his daughter a secretary. At one stage in the mid-1950s Bill junior opened the batting for St Kilda first XI, having earlier been a leg-spinner batting at number nine, 10 or 11 with University. Had St Kilda used him lower in the order he might have had a longer career because he found it difficult to open an innings after working all morning and then dashing across town to the game. 'Your future is in dentistry, not cricket,' his father advised. Bill junior took heed.

In the same era, when the VCA increased its selection committee from three members to five, Bill Woodfull and the Victorian skipper were added. Woodfull, in keeping with his resolve to focus his attention on his career, accepted the position for season 1955–56 but did not continue. His replacement, appropriately, was Bill Ponsford who did the job for the next three seasons. Ponsford was succeeded in 1959–60 by former Fitzroy wicketkeeper Bill Jacobs.

Ponsford's son Bill, who also worked for the State Bank where he rose to be a branch manager, emulated his father by playing District cricket with Melbourne although he is better remembered as a second XI rather than a first XI batsman. An opener, he was a member of Melbourne's seconds premiership teams in 1948–49 and 1956–57. His younger brother, Geoff, played in Melbourne's lower grade teams.

Around 1960 when Melbourne seconds cricketer Bob Hawke applied for membership of the MCC he was nominated by Bill Ponsford senior. Hawke's fondness for cricket has continued and more recently he revived the Prime Minister's XI match against touring teams in Canberra, which had lapsed after the retirement of Menzies.

Many people, both in Australia and overseas, were shocked on August 11 1965 when Bill Woodfull died suddenly while on holiday at Tweed Heads, Queensland. He was taking part in a golf tournament and was on the eighteenth fairway when he collapsed while suffering from a heart attack. A doctor arrived soon after, but heart massage and oxygen failed to revive him. Woodfull was 67. His funeral was held in Melbourne two days later.

On learning of Woodfull's death, Ponsford said his former opening partner had been a 'wonderful fighting cricketer'. He added: 'Bill was one of Australia's best captains with his team always right behind him. He will always remain in my memory as the man who handled the difficult situation of the bodyline series with tact and diplomacy.'

Victoria's Minister for Education, John Bloomfield, said Woodfull the teacher was just as accomplished and admirable as Woodfull the cricketer.

The Age devoted space on both the front and back page to record Woodfull's passing. In London, *The Times* ran a long obituary.

Despite the passage of time, the names Ponsford and Woodfull remained synonymous with cricket fame and reference was invariably made to them by students of the game. In 1971, in the jubilee issue of the magazine *Cricketer*, an exercise called 'The greatest of our time' was made by former Test stars Bill O'Reilly, Jack Fingleton, Les Ames and 'Gubby' Allen who named their top 20 cricketers from 1921–71.

All four judges chose Bradman, Compton, Hammond, Headley, Hobbs, Hutton, Lindwall, Sobers and Tate, while three included Bedser, Grimmett, Larwood, McCabe and O'Reilly (bearing in mind O'Reilly was humble enough not to choose himself). Ponsford was among those to receive two votes — from Fingleton and O'Reilly — in company with Godfrey Evans, Laker, Macartney, May, Miller and Worrell. Those to receive one vote were Duleepsinhji, Freeman, Neil Harvey, Hassett, Leyland, Mailey, Graeme Pollack, Rhodes, Barry Richards, Statham, Sutcliffe, Trueman, Weekes and Woolley.

After retiring from his job with the Melbourne Cricket Club in 1969, Bill Ponsford continued to live in South Caulfield. He and his wife Vera celebrated their golden wedding anniversary in 1974. Two other milestones followed: the Centenary Test at the MCG in 1977 to celebrate a century of Test cricket and the Lord's Centenary Test in 1980 to mark 100 years of Anglo-Australian Tests in England. Ponsford was among the special guests flown to England for the latter occasion where he met former rivals such as Andy Sandham and Percy Fender. At one particular function he noticed he had been seated between Bill Bowes and Geoff Boycott, but the thought of a Yorkshire accent on either side of him prompted 'Ponny' to switch the place names.

Vera Ponsford died late in 1977 and the following year Bill left the suburbs of Melbourne to live with his son Geoff and daughter-in-law Glenis at Woodend, midway between Melbourne and Bendigo. Despite his advancing years, Bill kept a large garden and an equally large hedge tidy with a suburban orderliness. Perhaps it was a result of the discipline and tidiness that studded his years on the cricket field.

Late in 1985 the first 120 inductees to the Sport Australia Hall of Fame were announced, one of whom was Bill Ponsford. The inductees were divided into eras — pre 1925, 1926–50, 1951–75 and 1976–85. Of eight cricketers chosen, only Ponsford and Sir Donald Bradman represented the 1926–50 era which was full of brilliant players. Those chosen pre 1925 were Frederick Spofforth and Victor Trumper and in the 1951–75 era Richie Benaud, Neil Harvey, Bob Simpson and Dennis Lillee were chosen.

Selection of Ponsford was both an honour and an accurate apprai-sal of his worth. Twelve months later Ponsford was again honoured when the Melbourne Cricket Club renamed the Western Stand at the MCG after him. In earlier days, grandstands at the ground had been named after individuals, such as Henry Harrison, Ben Wardill and Frank Grey Smith, but later buildings bore drab names as indi-cated by Southern, Northern and Western. Ponsford certainly deserved to have his name on a grandstand. After all, he had scored both of his quadruple centuries and both of his triple centuries on the MCG.

Shortly before his eighty-seventh birthday Ponsford showed his enthusiasm for cricket by accepting the Marylebone Cricket Club's invitation to attend the match at Lord's between the MCC and a World XI to celebrate the MCC's bicentenary. Every living player who had made a double century at Lord's was invited. Assured by his doctor that he was healthy enough to journey to the other side of the world, he flew to London with his sons Bill and Geoff to share the occasion with a lot of other cricket celebrities.

Gwen Woodfull, who became very friendly with Vera Ponsford and used to visit her when the husbands were away on cricket tours, is an active octogenarian living on the Mornington Peninsula. She enjoys reminiscing about the Ponsford-Woodfull era and prefers to remember the game as it was before one-day cricket made inroads into the grand summer game.

THE SUCCESSORS

MANY of the records established by Ponsford and Woodfull in first-class cricket remain intact more than half a century after their retirement and there is every chance that they will still be standing a century after the Victorian openers set them. Since the Ponsford-Woodfull era Australia has been blessed with some fine opening combinations from Brown and Fingleton to Morris and Barnes, McDonald and Burke, Lawry and Simpson, Lawry and Redpath, Redpath and Stackpole, and to a lesser extent, Wood and Laird and Marsh and Boon.

During Australia's convincing four-nil win in South Africa in 1935–36, Fingleton and Brown gave their side starts of 12, 93, 105, 17, 233, 99 and 162. Fingleton struck a purple patch at this stage, scoring a century in four successive Test innings embracing the South Africa series and the first Test in the 1936–37 series against England. Nevertheless, he wasn't as prolific as Ponsford or Woodfull. Brown, who continued his career after World War II, generally batted better overseas and scored 23 of his 39 first-class hundreds on foreign soil.

Morris and Barnes scored several century opening partnerships against England immediately after the war. Their combination was relatively brief and scarcely bears comparison with Ponsford and Woodfull although each had some abundant seasons. In little more than four years after the spring of 1946, Morris reeled off 35 first-class centuries and averaged just on 70 an innings. Although his consistency fell away later in his career, Morris finished with 46 centuries, an average of 53.67 and considerable praise as a great left-hand batsman from Sir Donald Bradman. Barnes, who had played one Test when war broke out, almost certainly would have enjoyed a much longer Test career had the game not been interrupted.

During the 1950s Colin McDonald and Jim Burke proved an industrious and at times fruitful pair of openers in an era when field placings were negative and scoring slow. Among their partnerships were 190 against South Africa in 1957–58, 171 against England the next season and an earlier stand of 137 against England. Burke, on one hand, a fine grafter of runs but on the other the despair of cricket watchers because of his slowness, had a highest Test score of 189 and once hit 220 for New South Wales against South Australia. Believe it or not he also hit a century before lunch against Somerset during Australia's tour of England in 1956.

McDonald, who once put on 337 with Ken Meuleman for the first wicket in a Victoria versus South Australia game, hit five Test centuries and another 17 half centuries. Like Woodfull he was an ideal opener, painstakingly removing the shine from the ball and making it easier for the number three and four batsmen.

The advent of Bill Lawry and Bob Simpson as an opening pair was a timely one. Simpson had proved a successful partner for McDonald against the West Indies in 1960–61, but dropped down the order to make way for Lawry in 1961 when the Victorian left-hander made his Test debut. Injury precluded McDonald from participating in the fourth Test, so Simpson opened with Lawry. Australia trailed by 177 on the first innings, which meant that Lawry and Simpson had to provide a century partnership in the second innings if Australia was to have any chance of getting back into the game. Their stand of 113 opened the way to a score of 432. Benaud followed with a match-winning six for 70 which gave Australia the Test and the Ashes.

Lawry and Simpson, who once shared a first-wicket stand of 382 against the West Indies in 1965, were associated in nine century partnerships in Tests. Ponsford and Woodfull had been involved in only three, but in all first-class games the former pair had 23 century partnerships compared to 20 by Lawry and Simpson. Both as a partnership and individually, Lawry and Simpson were outstanding.

Simpson, like Ponsford, had the extraordinary capacity and endurance to play marathon innings. He exceeded 300 once in a Test and once for New South Wales. Rushed into first-class cricket as a teenager, Simpson took time to mature. But at the age of 23 he had established himself as an opening batsman and eventually became a run machine. It was not unusual for him to average more than 60 in a season.

Lawry took little more than six months to advance from a useful Sheffield Shield player to a household name. His spectacular debut in England in 1961 was followed by consistent, albeit often dour scoring for the rest of the decade. Like Woodfull, he was a fine exponent of the opener's craft but unlike his predecessor the demands of captaincy didn't always rest comfortably on his shoulders.

Ian Redpath, who hit 97 and shared an opening stand of 219 with Lawry in his Test debut against South Africa in 1963–64, also shared a number of century starts with Lawry while representing Victoria. A steady, competent player rather than a run machine, Redpath had a fine temperament for an opener. His value to the Test team was underlined by the number of times he made a useful rather than a large score. In 67 Tests he hit eight centuries, but on 31 other occasions completed a half century.

Keith Stackpole, regular Test opener from the third Test of the 1968–69 series against the West Indies until his retirement at the end of the 1973–74 season, also gave good service to Victoria. Unlike many openers, Stackpole scored quickly at the start of an innings if he believed the runs were there. A good partner for the cautious left-hander Lawry, right-hander Stackpole was essentially a back-foot player while Lawry tended to play forward. Stackpole played the cut well and enjoyed the hook, despite the risk of a catch from both shots, which brought him many runs. One of the more exciting openers, he hit 22 first-class centuries including seven in Tests.

West Australian Graeme Wood also hit seven centuries in Tests, but after he and Bruce Laird had given Australia a start of 106 against New Zealand in Auckland in 1982, almost four years and more than 30 Tests passed before our openers managed a century partnership again. Tasmanian David Boon and West Australian Geoff Marsh broke the drought against India in the third Test in Sydney in January, 1986 when they started with 217. Yet 12 months later Boon's form was not good enough to warrant Test selection.

One of the major problems affecting Australia in Tests over the past decade has been the lack of a reliable pair of openers. Oh for another Lawry or Morris, or better still another Ponsford and Woodfull!

Comparing succeeding Test openers to Ponsford and Woodfull isn't easy in view of the many charges to the framework of the game over the past half century, but the career figures of the various leading players provide a common ground worthy of illustrating the value of Ponsford and Woodfull to Australian and Victorian teams:

	Inns.	N.O.	Runs	H.S.	Avg.	100s
W. Ponsford	235	23	13,819	437	65.18	47
W. Woodfull	245	39	13,388	284	64.99	49
J. Fingleton	166	13	6816	167	44.54	22
W. Brown	284	15	13,838	265*	57.44	39
A. Morris	250	15	12,614	290	53.67	46
S. Barnes	164	10	8333	234	54.11	26
C. McDonald	307	26	11,376	229	40.48	24
J. Burke	204	36	7563	220	45.01	21
W. Lawry	413	48	18,735	266	51.33	50
R. Simpson	436	62	21,029	359	56.22	60
I. Redpath	391	34	14,993	261	41.99	32
K. Stackpole	279	22	10,100	207	39.29	22

Perhaps the overriding feature of Ponsford and Woodfull when comparing them with their successors is that they were immensely popular with their followers. Successors have built imposing records, but have not had as much affection from the rank and file Australian. Therein lies the reason why the names William Harold Ponsford and William Maldon Woodfull are legendary.

STATISTICS

TEST RECORDS BY SERIES

BILL PONSFORD
versus England

	M.	Inns.	N.O.	H.S.	Runs	Av.	100s	50s
1924–25	5	10	-	128	468	46.80	2	1
1926	2	3	-	23	37	12.33	-	-
1928–29	2	3	1	6	13	6.50	-	-
1930	4	6	-	110	330	55.00	1	2
1932–33	3	6	-	85	141	23.50	-	1
1934	4	7	1	266	569	94.83	2	1
	20	35	2	266	1558	47.21	5	5

versus West Indies

	M.	Inns.	N.O.	H.S.	Runs	Av.	100s	50s
1930–31	5	7	1	183	467	77.83	2	1

versus South Africa

	M.	Inns.	N.O.	H.S.	Runs	Av.	100s	50s
1931–32	4	6	1	34	97	19.40	-	-
TOTALS	29	48	4	266	2122	48.22	7	6

BILL WOODFULL
versus England

	M.	Inns.	N.O.	H.S.	Runs	Av.	100s	50s
1926	5	6	-	141	306	51.00	2	-
1928–29	5	10	1	111	491	54.55	3	1
1930	5	7	1	155	345	57.50	1	3
1932–33	5	10	1	73*	305	33.88	-	3
1934	5	8	-	73	228	28.50	-	1
	25	41	3	155	1675	44.07	6	8

versus West Indies

	M.	Inns.	N.O.	H.S.	Runs	Av.	100s	50s
1930–31	5	6	-	83	204	34.00	-	2

versus South Africa

	M.	Inns.	N.O.	H.S.	Runs	Av.	100s	50s
1931–32	5	7	1	161	421	70.16	1	3
TOTALS	35	54	4	161	2300	46.00	7	13

FIRST-CLASS RECORD
(season by season)
BILL PONSFORD

	M.	Inn.	N.O.	Runs	H.S.	Av.	100s	50s
1920–21	1	2	-	25	19	12.50	-	-
1921–22	1	1	-	162	162	162.00	1	-
1922–23	3	4	-	616	429	154.00	2	1
1923–24	5	8	1	777	248	111.00	4	1
1924–25	10	18	-	926	166	51.44	3	4
1925–26	8	12	1	701	158	63.72	3	3
1926 (Aust. in England)								
	21	26	4	901	144	40.95	3	2
1926–27	6	10	-	1229	352	122.90	6	2
1927–28	6	8	-	1217	437	152.12	4	1
1927–28 (Aust. in NZ)								
	6	9	1	452	148	56.50	1	3
1928–29	5	8	3	448	275*	89.60	1	2
1929–30	10	16	-	729	166	45.56	3	2
1930 (Aust. in England)								
	24	33	4	1425	220*	49.13	4	6
1930–31	9	13	2	816	187	74.18	4	1
1931–32	9	15	2	399	134	30.69	1	1
1932–33	7	10	-	475	200	47.50	1	1
1933–34	8	13	1	606	122	50.50	1	4
1934 (Aust. in England)								
	22	27	4	1784	281*	77.56	5	7
1934–35	1	2	-	131	83	65.50	-	1
TOTALS	162	235	23	13,819	437	65.18	47	43
Tests	29	48	4	2122	266	48.22	7	6
Victoria	55	87	7	6902	437	86.27	26	17
Tour matches	63	79	12	3626	281*	54.11	10	15
(non-Tests)								
Aust. XI	10	12	-	747	166	62.25	3	3
(in Australia)								
Other games	5	9	-	422	131	46.88	1	2
TOTALS	162	235	23	13,819	437	65.18	47	43

BILL WOODFULL

	M.	Inn.	N.O.	Runs	H.S.	Av.	100s	50s
1921–22	2	2	-1	175	153	175.00	1	-
1922–23	6	11	3	598	123	74.75	2	3
1923–24	5	8	1	300	117	42.85	1	1
1924–25	5	10	2	494	120*	61.75	1	5
1924–25 (Victoria in NZ)								
	6	9	-	706	212*	176.50	3	3
1925–26	9	14	-	890	236	63.57	3	3
1926 (Aust. in England)								
	27	34	5	1672	201	57.65	8	6
1926–27	5	8	1	483	140	69.00	2	2
1927–28	5	7	2	645	191*	129.00	2	3
1927–28 (Aust. in NZ)								
	6	9	3	781	284	130.16	3	2
1928–29	8	13	3	854	275*	85.40	4	2
1929–30	5	6	3	231	100*	77.00	1	1
1930 (Aust. in England)								
	23	26	1	1434	216	57.36	6	6
1930–31	9	12	2	477	177	47.70	1	3
1931–32	9	15	2	849	161	65.30	3	4
1932–33	11	19	1	602	83	33.44	-	5
1933–34	10	14	1	818	129	62.92	4	3
1934 (Aust. in England)								
	22	27	3	1268	228*	52.83	3	6
1934–35	1	1	-	111	111	111.00	1	-
TOTALS	174	245	39	13,388	284	64.99	49	58
Tests	35	54	4	2300	161	46.00	7	13
Victoria	59	94	21	5484	275*	75.12	18	26
Tour matches	63	75	11	4276	284	66.81	17	16
(non-Tests, but excluding Vic. in NZ)								
Aust. IX (in Australia)	12	14	2	818	148	68.16	4	2
Other games	5	8	1	510	129	72.85	3	1
Totals	174	245	39	13,388	284	64.99	49	58

FIRST-CLASS CENTURIES

BILL PONSFORD (47)

162 Victoria versus Tasmania	Launceston	1921–22
429 Victoria versus Tasmania	Melbourne	1922–23
108 Victoria versus South Australia	Adelaide	1922–23
248 Victoria versus Queensland	Melbourne	1923–24
159 Victoria versus South Australia	Melbourne	1923–24
110 Victoria versus New South Wales	Sydney	1923–24
110n.o. Victoria versus New South Wales	Sydney	1923–24
166 Victoria versus South Australia	Adelaide	1924–25
110 Australia versus England (1st Test)	Sydney	1924–25
128 Australia versus England (2nd Test)	Melbourne	1924–25
158 Victoria versus Western Australia	Fitzroy	1925–26
138 Victoria versus New South Wales	Sydney	1925–26
102 Australian XI versus Western Australia	Perth	1925–26
110n.o. Australians versus MCC	Lord's	1926
143n.o. Australians versus Glamorgan	Swansea	1926
144 Australians versus Warwickshire	Birmingham	1926
151 Victoria versus Queensland	Melbourne	1926–27
131 Australian XI versus The Rest	Sydney	1926–27
214 Victoria versus South Australia	Adelaide	1926–27
352 Victoria versus New South Wales	Melbourne	1926–27
108 Victoria versus South Australia	Melbourne	1926–27
116 Victoria versus Queensland	Brisbane	1926–27
133 Victoria versus South Australia	Adelaide	1927–28
437 Victoria versus Queensland	Melbourne	1927–28
202 Victoria versus New South Wales	Melbourne	1927–28
336 Victoria versus South Australia	Melbourne	1927–28
148 Australians versus Otago	Dunedin	1927–28
275n.o. Victoria versus South Australia	Melbourne	1928–29
131 Ryder's XI versus Woodfull's XI	Sydney	1929–30
110 Victoria versus South Australia	Melbourne	1929–30
166 Australian XI versus Tasmania	Hobart	1929–30
131 Australians versus Derbyshire	Chesterfield	1930
220n.o. Australians versus Oxford University	Oxford	1930
143 Australians versus Yorkshire	Bradford	1930
110 Australia versus England (5th Test)	The Oval	1930
109n.o. Victoria versus New South Wales	Melbourne	1930–31
187 Victoria versus West Indians	Melbourne	1930–31
183 Australia versus West Indies (2nd Test)	Sydney	1930–31
109 Australia versus West Indies (3rd Test)	Brisbane	1930–31
134 Victoria versus South Australia	Adelaide	1931–32
200 Victoria versus New South Wales	Sydney	1932–33
122 Victoria versus South Australia	Adelaide	1933–34

229n.o. Australians versus Cambridge Univ.	Cambridge	1934
281n.o. Australians versus MCC	Lord's	1934
125 Australians versus Surrey	The Oval	1934
181 Australia versus England (4th Test)	Leeds	1934
266 Australia versus England (5th Test)	The Oval	1934

BILL WOODFULL (49)

153 Victoria versus Western Australia	Perth	1921–22
115 Victoria versus South Australia	Melbourne	1922–23
123 Victoria versus South Australia	Adelaide	1922–23
117 Victoria versus New South Wales	Melbourne	1923–24
120n.o. Victoria versus New South Wales	Sydney	1924–25
212n.o. Victoria versus Canterbury	Christchurch	1924–25
110n.o. Victoria versus New Zealanders	Wellington	1924–25
150n.o. Victoria versus New Zealanders	Christchurch	1924–25
236 Victoria versus South Australia	Melbourne	1925–26
126 Victoria versus New South Wales	Sydney	1925–26
148 Australian XI versus Tasmania	Launceston	1925–26
201 Australians versus Essex	Leyton	1926
118 Australians versus Surrey	The Oval	1926
100 Australians versus Middlesex	Lord's	1926
102n.o. Australians versus Nottinghamshire	Nottingham	1926
141 Australia versus England (3rd Test)	Leeds	1926
117 Australia versus England (4th Test)	Manchester	1926
156 Australians versus Surrey	The Oval	1926
116n.o. Australians versus An England XI	Blackpool	1926
133 Victoria versus New South Wales	Melbourne	1926–27
140 Australian XI versus the Rest	Sydney	1926–27
191n.o. Victoria versus New South Wales	Melbourne	1927–28
106 Victoria versus South Australia	Melbourne	1927–28
284 Australian XI versus New Zealand	Auckland	1927–28
165 Australians versus Wellington	Wellington	1927–28
107 Australians versus Otago	Dunedin	1927–28
111 Australia versus England (2nd Test)	Sydney	1928–29
107 Australia versus England (3rd Test)	Melbourne	1928–29
102 Australia versus England (5th Test)	Melbourne	1928–29
275n.o. Victoria versus MCC	Melbourne	1928–29
100n.o. Victoria versus MCC	Melbourne	1929–30
133 Australians versus Worcestershire	Worcester	1930
121 Australians versus Yorkshire	Sheffield	1930
216 Australians versus Cambridge University	Cambridge	1930
141 Australians versus Surrey	The Oval	1930
155 Australia versus England (2nd Test)	Lord's	1930
116 Australia versus Northamptonshire	Northampton	1930
177 Victoria versus South Australia	Adelaide	1930–31

147 Victoria versus New South Wales	Melbourne	1931–32
121 Victoria versus South Africaans	Melbourne	1931–32
161 Australia versus South Africa (3rd Test)	Melbourne	1931–32
129 Rest of Australia versus New South Wales	Sydney	1933–34
126 Australian XI versus Tasmania	Launceston	1933–34
124 Australian XI versus Tasmania	Hobart	1933–34
118 Woodfull's XI versus Richardson's XI	Melbourne	1933–34
172n.o. Australians versus Lancashire	Manchester	1934
131 Australians versus Gloucestershire	Bristol	1934
228n.o. Australians versus Glamorgan	Swansea	1934
111 Woodfull's XI versus Richardson's XI	Melbourne	1934–35

PONSFORD-WOODFULL CENTURY PARTNERSHIPS

First wicket (18):
375 Victoria versus NSW, MCG, 1926–27 (P.352, W.133)
236 Victoria versus South Australia, MCG, 1927–28 (P.336, W.106)
227 Victoria versus NSW, MCG, 1927–28 (P.202, W.99)
223 Australians versus The Rest, SCG, 1926–27 (P.131, W.140)
214 Australians versus Otago, Dunedin, 1927–28 (P.148, W.107)
184 Australian XI versus NZ, Auckland, 1927–28 (P.86, W.284)
183 Australians versus Gloucestershire, Bristol, 1934 (P.54, W.131)
162 Australia versus England, Lord's (2nd Test), 1930 (P.81, W.155)
159 Australia versus England, The Oval (5th Test), 1930 (P.110, W.54)
+158** Victoria versus South Africans, MCG, 1931–32 (P.84*, W.73*)
138 Victoria versus NSW, SCG, 1932–33 (P.200, W.78)
122 Australians versus Wellington, Wellington, 1927–28 (P.58, W.165)
118 Australians versus An England XI, Folkestone., 1930 (P.76, W.34)
117 Australians versus Warwickshire, Birmingham, 1926 (P.144, W.51)
115 Victoria versus Queensland, MCG, 1926–27 (P.151, W.56)
106 Australia versus England, Manchester (4th Test), 1930 (P.83, W.54)
+104 Victoria versus South Australia, MCG, 1926–27 (P.84, W.34)
104 Woodfull's XI versus Richardson's XI, MCG, 1933–34 (P.42, W.118)

Second wicket (1):
+109 Victoria versus South Australia, Adelaide, 1924–25 (P.77, W.67)

Fourth wicket (3):
+178 Victoria versus NSW, SCG, 1925–26 (P.138, W.126)
133 Victoria versus South Australia, Adelaide, 1922–23 (P.108, W.123)
132 Woodfull's XI versus Richardson's XI, MCG, 1934–35 (P.83, W.111)

Fifth wicket (1):
183 Australia versus West Indies, SCG (2nd Test), 1930–31 (P.183, W.58)

**Unfinished
+ Second innings.

METHOD OF DISMISSAL

BILL PONSFORD		BILL WOODFULL	
Bowled	71	Bowled	51
Caught	93	Caught	99
Caught & bowled	7	Caught & bowled	11
LBW	18	LBW	15
Run out	9	Run out	20
Stumped	10	Stumped	10
Hit wicket	4		

FIRST XI DISTRICT CRICKET

BILL PONSFORD

for St Kilda

	M.	Inns.	N.O.	Runs	H.S.	Av.	100s	50s
*1916–17	10	13	-	121	25	9.30	-	-
*1917–18	10	12	1	167	60	15.18	-	1
*1918–19	10	13	2	483	95	43.90	-	3
1919–20	11	12	1	303	94	27.54	-	2
1920–21	11	12	3	386	72*	42.88	-	3
1921–22	9	8	-	211	64	26.37	-	2
1922–23	9	10	1	329	99	36.55	-	3
1923–24	10	10	2	566	125	70.75	2	4
1924–25	5	6	-	291	108	48.50	1	2
1925–26	6	6	-	425	154	70.83	1	3
1926–27	7	8	1	779	295	111.28	3	1
1927–28	5	5	1	484	188	121.00	2	1
1928–29	3	2	-	131	77	65.50	-	2
1929–30	7	7	1	360	98	60.00	-	4
1930–31	4	4	-	303	148	75.75	2	-
TOTALS	117	128	13	5339	295	46.42	11	31

for Melbourne

	M.	Inns.	N.O.	Runs	H.S.	Av.	100s	50s
1931–32	6	6	1	269	161*	53.80	1	-
1932–33	5	5	1	353	136	88.25	1	2
1933–34	4	3	2	233	137*	233.00	1	1
1934–35	8	8	2	470	140	78.33	2	2
1935–36	12	14	3	829	175*	75.36	4	1
1936–37	8	7	1	337	100	56.16	1	2
1937–38	12	14	5	744	181*	82.66	3	1
TOTALS	55	57	15	3235	181*	77.02	13	9
GRAND TOTAL	172	185	28	8574	295	54.61	24	40

*Club matches only as District competition suspended during World War I

BILL WOODFULL

for Essendon

	M.	Inns	N.O.	Runs	H.S.	Av.	100s	50s
*1916–17	6	7	2	55	24*	11.00	-	-

for South Melbourne

	M.	Inns	N.O.	Runs	H.S.	Av.	100s	50s
1921–22	3	3	1	303	156*	151.50	1	2
1922–23	10	11	1	636	187	63.60	1	5
1923–24	9	9	2	340	139	48.57	1	1
TOTALS	22	23	4	1279	187	67.31	3	8

for Carlton

	M.	Inns	N.O.	Runs	H.S.	Av.	100s	50s
1924–25	4	4	1	161	118	53.70	1	-
1925–26	5	5	-	316	135	63.20	1	2
1926–27	5	6	1	457	142	91.40	3	2
1927–28	3	3	1	266	128*	133.00	1	2
1928–29	4	4	-	206	120	51.50	1	1
1929–30	3	3	2	287	132*	287.00	2	-
1930–31	3	3	-	66	36	22.00	-	-
1931–32	4	4	-	213	133	53.25	1	1
1932–33	2	3	2	144	56*	144.00	-	2
1933–34	4	4	2	317	132*	158.50	2	1
1934–35	4	4	-	201	105	50.25	1	1
1935–36	10	10	2	477	124*	59.62	1	3
TOTALS	51	53	11	3111	142	74.07	14	15
GRAND TOTAL	79	83	17	4445	187	67.35	17	23

*Club matches only as District competition suspended during World War I.

ACKNOWLEDGEMENTS

The Ponsford family for use of pictures on pages I (top), IV (bottom), V, VI (bottom), VII (top), VIII (bottom), IX, X, XI, XII and XIV.

Bill Woodfull jun. for use of pictures on pages I (bottom), VII (bottom), VIII (top), XIII and XV.

The *Herald and Weekly Times* for use of picture on page XVI.

Bill Ponsford for his time and insight into his career.
Geoff and Glenis Ponsford for their assistance.
Bill Woodfull jun. and Gwen Woodfull.
Ken Williams for his invaluable guidance on statistics.
Melbourne Cricket Club librarian Rex Harcourt for his co-operation, Victorian Cricket Association staff, J. B. Thomson, Leo O'Brien, Alan Chegwin, Olga Marion, Tom Leather and Norm Sowden.

BIBLIOGRAPHY

DERRIMAN, PHILIP, Bodyline.
DOUGLAS, CHRISTOPHER, Douglas Jardine. Spartan Cricketer.
DUNSTAN, KEITH, The Paddock That Grew.
MOYES, A. G., Australian Batsmen (from Charles Bannerman to Neil Harvey).
PAGE, MICHAEL, Bradman. The Illustrated Biography.
PERKINS, KEVIN. The Larwood Story.
PIESSE, KEN, Prahran Cricket Club Centenary History.
POLLARD, JACK, Australian Cricket, The Game and the Players.
ROBINSON, RAY, On Top Down Under, Australia's Cricket Captains.
ROSENWATER, IRVING, Sir Donald Bradman.
WHITTINGTON, R. S., and HELE, GEORGE, Bodyline Umpire.

The Age
The Argus
The Australasian
Ballarat Courier

Wisden
VCA annual reports

INDEX

149